Trees to Know
in Oregon and Washington

Edward C. Jensen
Author and photographer

Dedicated to Charles R. Ross, 1908–2006

EC 1450 • Revised December 2020 • SECOND PRINTING

"Northwest Forests" by Ralph E. Duddles, Allan Campbell III, Lou Torres, David A. Zahler, David Shaw and Edward C. Jensen
Illustrations by Hugh J. Hayes and Don Poole
Cover photo: Edward C. Jensen, Valley of the Giants Outstanding Natural Area, Oregon
Maps by Alan Dennis, OSU Extension Communications
Photos by Edward C. Jensen unless otherwise noted

Short history of *Trees to Know in Oregon*

Originally published January 1950
    Author: Charles R. Ross
    Artist: Hugh Hayes
Revised November 1957, May 1959, January/June/November 1966, June 1972
Revised March 1975, revised August 1978
Revised May 1994, revised June 2003
    Authors: Edward C. Jensen and Charles R. Ross
    Artist: Hugh J. Hayes
    Photographer: Edward C. Jensen
Revised April 2005
    Authors: Edward C. Jensen and Charles R. Ross
    Photographer: Edward C. Jensen
Revised November 2010
    Author: Edward C. Jensen
    Photographer: Edward C. Jensen

Ordering information

Visit catalog.extension.oregonstate.edu or call 1-800-561-6719

Oregon State University
Extension Service

Oregon State University Extension Service
422 Kerr Administration Building,
Corvallis OR 97331
catalog.extension.oregonstate.edu

ISBN-13: 978-0-87071-120-6
Library of Congress Control Number:
2020950274

The Library of Congress has cataloged the
2010 edition as follows:

Jensen, Edward C.
Trees to know in Oregon / principal author and photographer,
Edward C. Jensen ; illustrations by Hugh J. Hayes.—Rev. Nov.
2010.
    p. cm.—(EC ; 1450)
Rev. 60th anniversary ed.
Includes index.
ISBN 978-1-931979-25-2 (alk. paper)
1. Trees—Oregon—Identification. 2. Forests and forestry—
Oregon. I. Hayes, Hugh J. II. Campbell, Allan, 1936- Oregon's
forests. III. Oregon State University. Extension Service. IV. Title.
V. Series: EC (Oregon State University. Extension Service) ; 1450.

QK182.J45 2010
582.1609795—dc22   2010039995

Contents

"Happy is the man to whom every tree is a friend."

— John Muir, explorer and naturalist

The story behind the book

Trees *To Know* owes its origin to Charles R. Ross, Oregon State University Extension Forester from 1946 until his retirement in 1970. As a youth, Charlie developed a love of nature from a series of nature books for children in his home state of North Carolina — and he thought he should give the same gift to the children of Oregon. In 1950 his passion gave rise to the first edition of *Trees to Know in Oregon*. I've been fortunate to carry on his legacy since 1994.

In addition to his love of trees, Charlie was a prolific writer on land use and population issues. He was a staunch advocate for the importance of green space in our lives and was a founding member of the Greenbelt Land Trust in Corvallis.

This edition of *Trees To Know* expands its scope, and its title, to more clearly include Oregon, Washington, and the border areas of surrounding states and provinces. It includes a few more species of trees — including several rare species native to southwest Oregon.

The original edition of *Trees to Know*, published in 1950.

For these later species I owe a debt of gratitude to Frank Callahan, for sharing his in-depth knowledge and excellent photographs. This edition also updates several scientific names. Its section on Northwest forests has been expanded to include those of Washington, and it includes a new section on how Northwest forests are likely to be affected by changing climates.

Over the 70 years since its initial publication, *Trees to Know* has become a mainstay for 4-H and youth education, community college and university students, homeowners, gardeners, small woodland owners and visitors to the Pacific Northwest. Many editors and designers have combined efforts to make it the publication it is today. For the 2020 edition, Ariel Ginsburg served as editor and Janet Donnelly as designer. Maps are by Alan Dennis.

I owe a special debt of gratitude to my family (Linda, Chris, Nick and Courtney) for their extraordinary patience during a lifetime of family trips as I pulled off the road or took a sudden detour when just the right light was hitting a particular tree on the hillside.

To those mentioned here, to the many others who have helped along the way, and to some 10,000 OSU students who helped hone my knowledge of the Northwest's trees and shrubs, my sincerest thanks. I hope this new edition continues to serve you well.

— Edward C. Jensen

What to know about *Trees to Know*

Here's what you'll find in these pages:

- **This book focuses on trees native** to Pacific Northwest forests. Most trees described in this book are native to Oregon and Washington, but a few are naturalized. (Humans introduced them, but they escaped cultivation and now survive on their own.) All grow and reproduce without human intervention. There is a section near the back of the book on common non-native ornamental species, so those species are not included in the main section.

- **Geographically, this book covers most** of the Pacific Northwest. While its focus is on Oregon and Washington, this book also works well in northern California, southern British Columbia, the panhandle of Idaho and adjoining parts of western Montana. California has a rich and diverse flora, much of which is different from that of the Pacific Northwest; as a result, *many* California trees are not included in this book — only those that reach northward into Oregon. Many species in the book range even more widely than the Pacific Northwest, such as most of California or the Rocky Mountain complex. A few even extend into our northern or eastern forests.

- **The Pacific Northwest is home to many shrubs** that grow tall enough to be considered trees (although they typically have multiple stems) and a few that sometimes grow with a single stem (like a tree). As a result, several species included in this book are also covered in *Shrubs to Know in Pacific Northwest Forests*, also available from OSU Extension.

- **Most trees in this book are described at the species level,** but several are described at the variety level when it seems more appropriate. The section on willows emphasizes genus-level characteristics rather than species characteristics because there are so many, and the characteristics separating species are often minor or intergrade between species. In the field, most folks are happy stopping at the genus level for willows.

- **Trees in this book are arranged alphabetically** by the common name of the genus — cypresses, Douglas-firs, false cedars, etc. That's the name that most readers will be familiar with.

Approximate area covered by this book

Shaded areas indicate forested lands. Some trees venture into adjoining rangelands, often along streams or on moist slopes. Many species in this book range much more widely than the area shown in this map — spanning the West, or even large parts of North America.

A word about poisonoak and poison ivy

Don't go into the woods before learning to identify these common plants. Exposure to Pacific poisonoak or Western poison ivy provokes uncomfortable allergic reactions. Here's what you need to know.

Pacific poisonoak or poisonoak

Toxicodendron diversilobum • Formerly *Rhus diversiloba*

Pacific poisonoak is not really an oak. (Its fruit is not an acorn.) Therefore, its common name is correctly written either as one word (poisonoak) or hyphenated (poison-oak) to distinguish it from true oaks.

Pacific poisonoak 'leaves of three'

Itch, itch, itch. Poisonoak contains a chemical (urushiol) that gives most people an itchy rash when they touch it. All parts of the plant — leaves, stems, flowers, fruits and roots — contain urushiol, so no part is safe to touch. And because the chemical is present throughout the year, you must always be careful around poisonoak. Many people develop a rash after handling a pet that has walked through a patch of poisonoak, and some even get it from the smoke of burning plants.

Leaves of three — let it be. Poisonoak leaves are pinnately compound with three (and occasionally five) leaflets per leaf, but the leaflets may range dramatically in size and shape. When growing in the sun, they are commonly 2 to 3 inches long, but in shade they may reach 6 inches long. Their margins are wavy and irregularly lobed; the lateral leaflets often have several lobes on their outer edge and no lobes on the inner edge. Their leaves turn beautiful reds and yellows in the fall. Poisonoak has three diverse growth forms: it can grow as an upright shrub, crawl along the ground, or climb high into trees, sending down long, thin branches to "catch" those passing by.

Range and habitat. Poisonoak grows primarily at low elevations on the west side of the Cascades and Sierra Nevada from southern British Columbia through southern California. It is probably the most common shrub in California. It grows in both sun and shade but is especially fond of dry conifer sites, oak woodlands and chaparral brushfields.

Folklore about poisonoak. Folklore suggests that chewing a poisonoak leaf when you're young will make you resistant to its toxin. DON'T BELIEVE IT — you're likely to end up with a terrible rash — inside and out! Some people seem to have a natural immunity to poisonoak, but

HABIT: Grows as an upright shrub to several feet tall, or as a trailing or climbing vine up to 50' tall.

LEAVES: Pinnately compound (usually in threes but sometimes fives), alternate and deciduous. Wavy margins with irregular lobes, but sometimes unlobed. Size of leaflets varies, commonly 2–3" long, but up to 6" in shade.

TWIGS: Slender, tan. May have grasping tendrils. Have naked buds (no scales).

FLOWERS AND FRUIT: Flowers are small, clustered and inconspicuous; greenish-yellow in color. Fruits are small white drupes with fine, black lines.

most don't. Also, immunity may change with your age and exposure to the plant. Learn to recognize poisonoak and then protect yourself by wearing long clothing or by avoiding it altogether. And always wash with hot, soapy water if you happen to contact it.

Member of the cashew family. Interestingly, poisonoak, poison ivy and poison sumac are all members of the cashew family.

Western poison ivy or poison ivy

Toxicodendron rydbergii • Formerly *Rhus radicans*

Scratch, scratch, scratch. Like Pacific poisonoak, western poison ivy gives most people an itchy rash when they touch it. All parts of the plant — leaves, stems, flowers, fruits and roots — contain an irritating chemical (urushiol), so no part is safe to touch. And because urushiol is present throughout the year, you must always be careful around poison ivy. Many people are so allergic that they develop a rash after handling a pet that has walked through a patch of poison ivy, and some even get it from the smoke of burning plants. Because "ivy" is not a specific genus of plant, writing "poison ivy" as two separate words is correct (as opposed to poisonoak, in which the two words should be joined or hyphenated.)

PHOTO: JOE MONTGOMERY
Western poison ivy

Leaves of three — let it be. Western poison ivy leaves are quite similar to those of Pacific poisonoak — they are pinnately compound with three leaflets per leaf (almost never 5). When growing in the sun, the leaflets are commonly 2 to 3 inches long but in shade may reach 6 inches long. Their margins are wavy and irregularly lobed, often with several lobes on the outer edge and no lobes on the inner edge. Their leaflets are typically more pointed than those of Pacific poisonoak. Their leaves turn beautiful reds and yellows in the fall. Western poison ivy grows primarily as an upright shrub (typically 3 to 10 feet tall), not as a climbing vine.

Range and habitat. Western poison ivy is native to most of Canada and the United States. In the Pacific Northwest it grows primarily east of the Cascade crest, from the lowlands well up mountain slopes; it does not occur in California. It can be found in forests and woodlands, near rivers and streams, along roads and on rocky banks. In eastern North America, it often grows in association with eastern poison ivy.

Folklore about poison ivy. As with poisonoak, folklore about poison ivy says that eating a leaf when you're young will make you resistant to its toxin. DON'T BELIEVE IT! Some people seem to have a natural immunity to poisonoak and poison ivy, but most don't. Also, immunity may change with your age and exposure to the chemical. Learn to recognize both poisonoak (especially west of the Cascades) and western poison ivy (especially east of the Cascades), and then protect yourself by wearing long clothing or by avoiding it altogether.

HABIT: Grows primarily as upright shrub, typically 3–10' tall. Sometimes sprawling or vinelike.

LEAVES: Pinnately compound (usually in threes), alternate and deciduous. The size of leaflets varies dramatically (2–6" long). The two lateral leaflets are asymmetrical and irregularly lobed; the terminal leaflet is symmetrical and more uniformly lobed or toothed.

TWIGS: Slender with naked buds. They lack tendrils, so they don't climb.

FLOWERS AND FRUIT: Flowers are small but densely clustered. Male and female flowers typically occur on separate plants. Fruits are small, white drupes that hang in grapelike clusters. Both flowers and fruits are toxic.

What is a tree?

What is a tree and what's not a tree is often intuitively obvious — but there are small trees and there are large shrubs, so there's still a lot of wiggle room. Although there's no single definition accepted by all, here's the gist of it:

Tree? Or shrub? One of our most common shrubs, vine maple, growing beneath one of our most common trees, Douglas-fir.

- **Trees are woody, perennial plants.** They have woody stems and woody roots, and they typically live several decades, or much longer in some cases. The oldest known tree, a bristlecone pine named Methuselah, lived 4,850 years!

- **Trees typically have a single stem** (commonly called a trunk), although some species commonly sprout from their base and so may have multiple trunks. (Pacific madrone and tanoak are two good examples from Pacific Northwest forests.)

- **Trees are typically at least 20 feet tall** at maturity, although a few are shorter. Some get MUCH taller — for example, in 2013 the coast redwood called Hyperion was measured at 379.7 feet tall.

- **Trees typically have trunks** that are over 6 inches in diameter when measured 4.5 feet above the ground (called breast height). Most grow much larger in the right environments. The giant sequoia General Sherman is over 32 feet in diameter!

- **The crowns of trees** often have characteristic shapes when grown in the open — determined by genetics, their environment, and how they react to competition for sunlight. When grown inside a forest, where they compete with other trees for light, they take on diverse shapes. In windy areas, like along the coast, they are often contorted into fanciful shapes.

So, follow this basic definition but don't be overly concerned about its strict application.

Trees are typically the defining components of Pacific Northwest forests. They are integral to these forests' many uses and values — including wood, water, wildlife, and recreation — and absolutely critical to how forests function ecologically.

How to be a tree detective

Identifying trees is a lot like identifying people. You can easily recognize a close friend, even if you catch only a glimpse. In fact, you can often recognize a friend from a fast-moving car, or even from a picture in a photo album when the friend was a different age or had a different hairstyle. However, if you meet a room full of strangers, you need to concentrate on specific characteristics before you can begin to tell individuals apart. And even then, you might struggle to remember their names.

It's the same with trees and other forest plants. When you know a tree well, you'll be able to identify and name it whether you see its leaves, its fruit, its flowers, or even its shape and color. When you know it well enough, you'll be able to recognize it in different stages of growth, in different locations, and even from fast-moving cars. You're likely to start by learning its common name, but may eventually want to learn its formal or scientific name, which is written in Latin to aid in worldwide communication about trees.

How can you get to know trees that well? First, learn to identify their most important characteristics, such as leaves, flowers and fruits. As you become better acquainted, examine each tree more carefully. Look at its bark, branching pattern, color and shape. Eventually, you may even get to know trees by where they live.

This book can help you start to know common forest trees of the Pacific Northwest. Keep it handy and take it with you on hikes. You'll be surprised how easy it is to learn the most common trees — and how much fun it is to improve your ability each time out.

How can you get to know trees? First, learn to identify the most important characteristics, such as leaves, flowers and fruits.

You can improve your ability to identify trees each time you visit the forest.

Common and scientific names of trees

Tree names can be confusing until you understand how they're developed. All plants have two kinds of names: common names and scientific names. Common names are written in English in English-speaking countries, German in Germany, Chinese in China, and so on. Scientific names are always written in Latin, so they can be used anywhere in the world.

Scientific names are governed by strict rules set by the International Botanical Congress. In theory, each plant has only one accepted scientific name. However, taxonomists sometimes differ over what scientific name should be applied to a particular plant, so there may be more than one name in use at the same time for the same plant. These are referred to as "synonyms" — different names for the same plant. Also, some taxonomists are "lumpers" (they prefer to group as many plants together as they can), and others are "splitters" (they prefer to separate plants on the basis of smaller characteristics). This also results in differences of opinion about what a particular plant should be called; synonyms also come into play here. Our improving ability to look at a tree's chemistry and genetics is leading to a better understanding of what's related to what — but it has also resulted in a flurry of new names.

Common names are usually easier to remember and use than scientific names, but they are developed much differently. Common names are derived in many ways: a characteristic of the plant (bigleaf maple or red alder), the geographic location in which it grows (Pacific madrone or Rocky Mountain maple), the area where it was first identified and categorized by Euro-Americans (Alaska-cedar or Utah juniper), the habitat in which it grows (subalpine fir), or a person's name (Douglas-fir), to name but a few.

There are few rules for assigning common names, and no one determines which common names are correct. Most often, local conventions rule. A tree can have many common names, and these names may reflect different countries or regions, growth stages, uses, or growth characteristics. For example, ponderosa pine is also called western yellow pine, bull pine, blackjack pine, rock pine, pinabete, pino real and pondosa pine, among others. However, its scientific name is always *Pinus ponderosa*. The shrub *Vaccinium membranaceum* is called thinleaf huckleberry, mountain huckleberry, black huckleberry, blue huckleberry, big huckleberry, big huck, square-twig huckleberry, mountain blueberry, mountain bilberry, twin-leaved huckleberry and big whortleberry. Some of these names are also applied to related species, which adds to the confusion of common names.

Trees belong to many different categories called taxa. (A single unit of a taxa is called a taxon.) The study of taxa is called taxonomy, and people who study taxonomy are called taxonomists. The most commonly used taxa for identifying trees and shrubs are genus and species. A genus is composed of species with similar characteristics, and a family is composed of genera with similar characteristics. All species can also be subdivided into varieties (var.) or subspecies (ssp.). Although the distinction between varieties and subspecies is useful for taxonomists, it is confusing to most others. In this book, varieties and subspecies are mentioned only when they are prominent in a region, and no specific distinction is made between the two taxa. It might also be worth noting that the word species is both singular and plural.

A scientific name for a particular species has two parts: the genus followed by a specific epithet (together they form the species' name). The genus refers to the general type of plant, and the specific epithet refers to one particular species within that genus. For example, the genus for maple is *Acer*, and the specific epithet for bigleaf maple is *macrophyllum*, so the scientific name for the bigleaf maple species is *Acer macrophyllum*.

How common and scientific names fit together

Type of name	Genus	Specific epithet	Species name
Common name	maple	bigleaf	bigleaf maple
Scientific name	*Acer*	*macrophyllum*	*Acer macrophyllum*

Because it always has two parts, this type of name is called a Latin binomial.

Common names generally work the same way. In the case of bigleaf maple, "maple" refers to the genus, and "bigleaf maple" refers to the particular species of maple.

Other maples have the same genus name but different species names. For example:

VINE MAPLE: *Acer circinatum*

ROCKY MOUNTAIN MAPLE: *Acer glabrum*

DOUGLAS MAPLE (a particular variety of Rocky Mountain maple): *Acer glabrum* var. *douglasii*

However, some common names have only one word (for example, snowbrush), and some have more than two (western wayfaring tree). Hyphenated common names indicate that the plant is not what its name implies. Examples from the tree world include Douglas-fir, which is not a fir (firs are in the genus *Abies,* but Douglas-firs are in the genus *Pseudotsuga*), and incense-cedar, which is not a cedar (cedars are in the genus *Cedrus*, but incense-cedar is in the genus *Calocedrus*). Examples from the shrub world include poisonoak, which is not an oak (oaks are in the genus *Quercus*, but poisonoak is in the genus *Toxicodendron*), and Indian-plum, which is not a plum (plums are in the genus *Prunus*, but Indian-plum is in the genus *Oemleria*). Sometimes hyphens are omitted and the two words are joined together if they are easy to read that way.

Poisonoak and poison-oak are both correct (that is, they are synonyms). But "poison oak" is not correct. (It implies that the plant is a particular kind of oak, which it is not.)

Although this naming system can take a while to get used to, you'll soon realize that learning plant names can be fun. They often tell you something special about the plant, such as who discovered it, a particular characteristic, or where it grows. When you encounter a new plant, see what you can learn from its name.

'Native' trees vs. 'naturalized' — and what do we mean by 'ornamental'?

- **Native plants** are those that inhabit an area without having been brought there by humans. Some may have developed in a particular location; others may have migrated from surrounding areas in response to natural influences such as climate change or the rise and fall of mountain ranges. Endemic is a more formal word for native and means the same thing.

- **Naturalized plants** are those that have been introduced into an area by humans and, once there, have been able to reproduce and survive on their own without human assistance. Naturalized plants are often referred to as exotics.

- **Invasive plants** are naturalized plants that spread rapidly, often overwhelming native plants. Sometimes native plants that rapidly expand into new areas — perhaps as a result of human-caused changes — are also said to be invasive. One example is western juniper, which invades native grasslands where humans have suppressed fires.

- **Ornamental and horticultural plants** are those that humans find useful in beautifying their own managed environments or in growing for economic purposes. Ornamentals can be native or non-native. Depending on the species and environment, they can also be highly invasive or remain where they are planted.

How trees reproduce

The ability of trees to reproduce is crucial to their success in nature.

SEXUAL REPRODUCTION: Nearly all trees can reproduce sexually (from seeds) — except for a very few that are bred by humans — but some are far more successful at it than others. The type of fruit produced, its abundance, and how it's distributed are all important to successful reproduction. Germination and early survival are also critical. Some species need a cold, moist period to germinate; others need exposure to heat or digestion by an animal; others need exposure to a certain light regime.

VEGETATIVE REPRODUCTION: Many trees, especially broadleaves, can also reproduce vegetatively (for example, by sprouting or layering). Depending on the species, trees can sprout from their base (where the top of the plant joins the root system), roots, underground burls, or even underground stems called rhizomes. Some trees also have the ability to layer, which means that new roots and stems form on branches that bend over, touch the ground, and become buried by forest litter, a fallen branch, or even snow.

How fire shapes our forests

PHOTO: U.S. FOREST SERVICE

HOW TREES RESPOND TO FIRE is of increasing interest to those who seek to understand how both managed and unmanaged forest ecosystems function. In general, fire damages the aboveground portions of woody plants, but some plants are more resistant to fire than others. The underground portions respond in a variety of ways, ranging from death to very aggressive sprouting from root collars, burls, roots and rhizomes. The response of trees to fire often determines the species composition and structure of forested landscapes for many decades.

Pause before you take a bite of any plant

Use caution when eating or even tasting unfamiliar plants.

Some are delicious, but others can give you an allergic reaction or make you violently ill. Some are toxic when eaten raw but edible when cooked. Some toxic plants resemble others that are edible.

You'd miss much of the joy of native plants by never eating any of them, so the species descriptions in this book often include notes about what is edible. But again, taste with caution until you're certain about the identity of a plant.

Exploring some traditional uses of plants

How people who came before us used plants is often of great interest to those who love native plants.

Though I'm not an expert in that field, I've tried to share some information from published literature on how Indigenous people and early settlers of the Pacific Northwest have used native plants. Both groups used native plants for food, medicine, clothing, tools and other necessities. Indigenous people continue these practices today. Uses often vary widely, especially for widespread trees and other plants.

Although many people may have used the same plant for medicine, they may have used it in different ways and at different dosages. In fact, it may have been helpful at one dose but harmful at a higher dose. I strongly discourage experimenting with medicinal use of plants unless you're with an expert.

Because of space limitations, I've greatly simplified what could be long and varied lists of uses of native plants.

What is range?

RANGE describes the geographic area over which a tree occurs. It's often described in terms of geographic boundaries, such as states and countries, or natural barriers, such as oceans, major rivers and mountain ranges. Ranges described in this book are indicators of where you can expect to find specific trees, but they do not imply absolute locations and boundaries.

PHOTO: JANET DONNELLY, © OREGON STATE UNIVERSITY

What is habitat?

HABITATS are specific types of places within larger geographic ranges where you can expect to find certain trees — along a stream, on a dry ridge, or on well-drained soils, for example. Some species have very specific requirements and occur only on sites that meet those requirements; these are often referred to as niche-specific species. Other species can grow under a wide range of conditions; these are said to have wide ecological amplitude. Habitat information is often very helpful in identifying trees, and experience will help you use this information successfully.

Know your tree terms

Trees are woody plants that typically have one main stem, called a trunk, and are over 20 feet tall at maturity. Shrubs, on the other hand, are woody plants that typically have multiple stems and are less than 20 feet tall at maturity. Although there are exceptions to this, it's a good rule of thumb.

The trees of Oregon and Washington fit into two major categories: conifers and broadleaves. Conifers have needlelike or scalelike leaves and usually bear seeds inside woody cones. Conifers are often called evergreens because most hold their leaves all year long; however, some conifers are deciduous — they drop their leaves in winter. All conifers are also called softwoods because their wood is relatively soft when compared with that of other trees.

Broadleaved trees, or broadleaves, usually have wide, flat leaves and bear their seeds inside soft fruits. All broadleaved trees are referred to as hardwoods because their wood generally is harder than that of conifers. A few, however, like cottonwoods and balsa, have very soft wood. Most broadleaved trees are deciduous — that is, they drop their leaves in winter — but a few are evergreen.

The following diagram may help you understand the relationship between these terms.

Conifers are often called evergreens because most hold their leaves all year long; however, some conifers are deciduous.

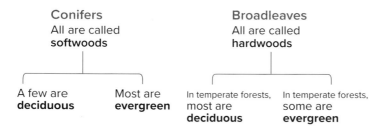

Conifers
All are called
softwoods

A few are
deciduous

Most are
evergreen

Broadleaves
All are called
hardwoods

In temperate forests, most are **deciduous**

In temperate forests, some are **evergreen**

Thousands of terms are used to describe trees. Luckily, we need only a few to begin identifying trees successfully.

Trees and groups of trees

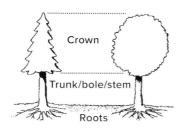

Crown

Trunk/bole/stem

Roots

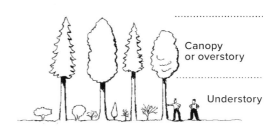

Canopy or overstory

Understory

Leaf and branching patterns

Alternate

Buds   Leaves

Opposite

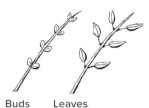

Buds   Leaves

Whorled

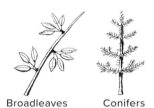

Broadleaves   Conifers

Parts of a leaf

Apex (tip)

Margin (edge)

Veins

Base (bottom)

Petiole

Stipules (only on some leaves)

Twig

Leaf types and arrangements

Broadleaves

Simple

Pinnately compound   Palmately compound

Conifers

Two-ranked

Spirally arranged

 Massed

Clusters/bundles/ fascicles

Leaf shapes

Broadleaves

Lance-shaped (Lanceolate)   Egg-shaped (Ovate)

Reverse egg-shaped (Obovate)   Elliptical/ oblong

Needle-like

Linear

Scale-like   Awl-like

Leaf margins

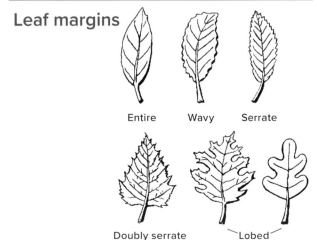

Entire   Wavy   Serrate

Doubly serrate   Lobed

Leaf tips and bases

Tips

Acute (pointed)

Rounded (blunt)

Notched   Truncated (cut off)

Bases

Asymmetrical (uneven)   Truncated (cut off)

Leaf veins

Pinnate

Arcuate (curved)

Palmate

Fruits

Cones

Dry fruits

Single samara   Double samara

Legume   Acorn   Nut

Fleshy fruits

Drupe (1 seed)   Berry (many seeds)

Pome (apple, pear)

Twigs

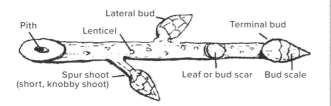

Pith   Lateral bud   Lenticel   Terminal bud   Spur shoot (short, knobby shoot)   Leaf or bud scar   Bud scale

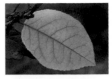

The key to successful identification

Fortunately, we don't need to remember all the characteristics of every tree. Keys help us make the most important distinctions. Keys come in all shapes and sizes. Some are based on pictures and some are based on words; some cover only trees while others cover only wildflowers; some are simple to use and some are very difficult. Most help us divide plants into two groups — those that have a particular characteristic and those that don't have it. If any group of plants is split often enough, eventually there will be only one plant left. If the key is accurate, and if we've made good decisions along the way, we'll have correctly identified the plant.

Using a key is like following the branches of a tree — each additional branch gets smaller and smaller until you reach a single branch tip. All the species described in a key are represented by the trunk, while each branch tip represents a single species of tree.

This book contains two keys: for conifers (page 18) and for broadleaved trees (page 75). They work exactly the same way, although the broadleaf key is longer because it contains more trees. To identify a plant, first decide whether the tree you want to identify is a conifer or a broadleaf. Then turn to the appropriate key.

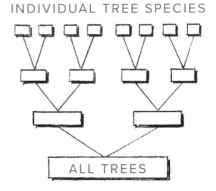

A place where conifers thrive

In Oregon and Washington, the diverse topography and climate combine to create a variety of habitats in which conifers thrive. Nearly 30 species of conifers are native to this region. Though most have leaves shaped like needles with tips that range from very sharp to blunt, a few have leaves shaped like overlapping scales (like shingles on a roof or scales on a fish).

Conifers grow especially well on the west slopes of the Cascades and throughout the Coast Range, where relatively warm temperatures and abundant rainfall allow them to grow even in winter. Different species of conifers also grow well on the east side of the Cascades because their needlelike leaves have small surface areas and thick, waxy coverings that help the trees retain moisture during the hot, dry summers and cold, dry winters. Conifers also grow well at high elevations because their evergreen nature allows them to begin growing in the spring as soon as temperatures rise above freezing.

Northwestern conifers can be grouped into about 14 different genera based on the structure of their "flowers" and fruit (the exact number depends a bit on who's doing the classification). The genera with needlelike leaves include Douglas-fir, pine, fir, spruce, larch, hemlock, redwood and yew. Those with scalelike leaves include cypress, arborvitae (the Northwest's single species is called redcedar), incense-cedar, white-cedar (the Northwest's single species is called Port-Orford-cedar), Nootka cypress (the Northwest's single species is Alaska-cedar) and juniper.

To identify conifers native to the Northwest, turn to the key on the next page. To learn more about the forests that these trees comprise, turn to "Northwest forests" on page 138.

Mountain hemlock, a common subalpine tree in the Northwest

PHOTO: U.S. FOREST SERVICE

Key to common native conifers of the Pacific Northwest*

To use this key

1. Begin with a tree, or a section of branch with needles or leaves.

2. Start at the top. Read the two statements directly below the starting point.

3. Decide which of the two statements (or drawings) better describes the tree. Then read the two statements directly under that box and make the same type of decision.

4. Continue until you've identified a single group of trees (called a genus). Turn to the page indicated and read the descriptions of individual species within that genus.

5. If the species description matches the tree you're trying to identify — GREAT! If it doesn't match, go back to start and try again.

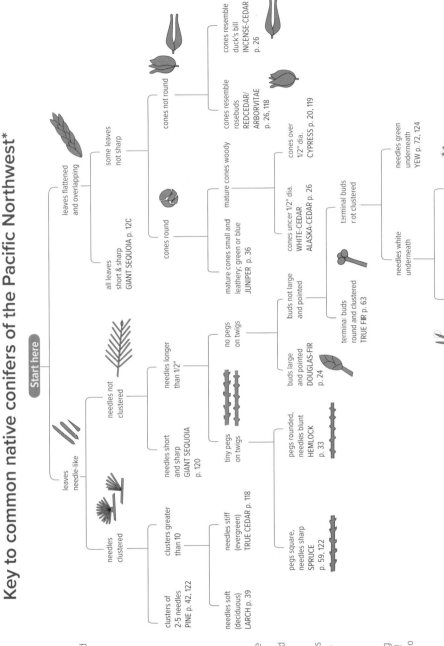

Start here

- leaves needle-like
  - needles clustered
    - clusters greater than 10
      - clusters of 2-5 needles PINE p. 42, 122
      - needles stiff (evergreen) TRUE CEDAR p. 118
      - needles soft (deciduous) LARCH p. 39
    - needles short and sharp GIANT SEQUOIA p. 120
  - needles not clustered
    - needles longer than 1/2"
      - no pegs on twigs
        - buds not large and pointed
          - terminal buds round and clustered TRUE FIR p. 63
          - terminal buds not clustered
            - needles white underneath
              - needles pointed REDWOOD p. 57
              - needles blunt HEMLOCK p. 33
            - needles green underneath YEW p. 72, 124
        - buds large and pointed DOUGLAS-FIR p. 24
      - tiny pegs on twigs
        - pegs rounded, needles blunt HEMLOCK p. 33
        - pegs square, needles sharp SPRUCE p. 59, 122

- leaves flattened and overlapping
  - all leaves short & sharp GIANT SEQUOIA p. 12C
  - some leaves not sharp
    - cones round
      - mature cones small and leathery; green or blue JUNIPER p. 36
      - mature cones woody
        - cones under 1/2" dia. WHITE-CEDAR ALASKA-CEDAR p. 26
        - cones over 1/2" dia. CYPRESS p. 20, 119
    - cones not round
      - cones resemble rosebuds REDCEDAR/ARBORVITAE p. 26, 118
      - cones resemble duck's bill INCENSE-CEDAR p. 26

Conifers from all over the world are planted and grow in the mild climate of the Pacific Northwest. This key focuses on trees that are native to the Northwest — that is, they arrived here on their own and grow without human assistance.

Cypresses *Cupressus* or *Hesperocyparis*

This is a confusing genus, any way you look at it. The common name, "cypress" is used for at least a dozen different genera throughout the world. Some taxonomists include all the true cypresses in the genus *Cupressus*, while others split them into some combination of *Cupressus*, *Hesperocyparis*, *Callitropsis*, and *Xanthocyparis*. New molecular evidence suggests that cypresses of the Old World be classified as *Cupressus*, while cypresses of the New World be classified as *Hesperocyparis*. However, molecular differences cannot be seen by the human eye, so other taxonomists argue that *Cupressus* should not be separated into multiple genera. Choosing to be a lumper, rather than a splitter, I've chosen to stick with the more traditional *Cupressus* for this edition of *Trees to Know*; perhaps that will change in the future.

There are approximately 25 species of *Cupressus* in the world, with about 15 in North America. Of these 15, nearly a dozen occur in California, with several occurring only in California. Four species (Baker's, McNab's, pygmy, and Sargent's) just barely cross the northern border of California into southwestern Oregon, where they reside in small groups or as scattered individuals. As a result, they are all subject to high risk of loss —from wildfire, flash floods, high winds, firewood cutting and the like. Rather than new species to the Northwest, they all appear to be "leftovers" from long ago when they were part of a larger, more contiguous Californian flora that extended into southwestern Oregon.

All four Oregon cypresses share a small stature; scale-like leaves; round, woody cones; and a tendency to grow on harsh sites; as a result, they are difficult to distinguish from one another. To make identification even more difficult, many cypresses also resemble junipers, but if you can find cones, the distinction is clear — cypresses have round, woody cones, usually ½ to 2 inches in diameter — junipers have smaller, round, colorful, berry-like cones (usually green, blue, or reddish-brown). Both cypresses and junipers have scale-like needles, but junipers often have sharp-pointed (awl-like) needles mixed in with their scale-like leaves; cypresses have far fewer awl-like needles, if any. Many other species of cypresses are planted as ornamentals throughout the Northwest, especially on sites where water is limited; but they can all be identified by their scale-like foliage and round, woody cones.

McNab's cypress is found in a few scattered areas of southwestern Oregon, below 4,000 feet.

▲ Baker's cypress

★ Sargent's cypress

● Pygmy cypress

◆ McNab's cypress

A quick comparison of Oregon cypresses

Note: Characteristics may intergrade and be less distinct than described below

Trees	Leaves	Cones
Baker's cypress	Distinct white resin dots.	Scales covered with warty, resinous bumps.
MacNab's cypress	Resin dots and bloom. Arrayed in flattened sprays (the only one to do so).	Commonly have distinct hornlike projections.
Pygmy cypress	Green without bloom or waxy resin.	Scales smooth with one distinct projection in center of scale.
Sargent's cypress	Whitish bloom but no resin dots.	Commonly borne on a distinct stalk; scales commonly blistered.

Baker's cypress

Cupressus bakeri or *Hesperocyparis bakeri*

Also called Modoc and Siskiyou cypress. Although this cypress is much more common in northeastern California than in southern Oregon, it is by far the most common of Oregon's four cypresses. It is a small-to-medium size tree that grows on harsh, dry sites characterized by serpentine soils (a group of minerals, often greenish or mottled, that are high in magnesium). It also grows on old lava flows and in the chaparral. Because mature trees have a conical crown, it is the most snow-tolerant of our cypresses, and may grow at elevations as high as 6,000 feet. Because of such harsh conditions, it grows slowly and occurs in small, scattered groups rather than closed forests.

Characteristics. Baker's cypress seldom exceeds 75 feet tall and 20 inches in diameter. Foliage is sparse and typically hangs down from the branches. Foliage is mostly scale-like (except that juvenile foliage may be sharp-pointed) and grows in opposing pairs (with leaves and branchlets opposite one another). It tends to be gray-green and has a distinct white resin dot on the back side of each tiny leaf. Cones are small, round and woody with 6 to 8 scales covered with warty bumps; initially green, they turn brown, then gray as they mature. Most are serotinous — that is, mature cones remain on the tree until they are opened by high heat or fire. Mature bark is thin and peeling in short curls.

Baker's cypress from its northernmost stand in the southern Oregon Cascades

McNab's cypress

Cupressus macnabiana or *Hesperocyparis macnabiana*

Common in California. In California, this is a fairly common cypress growing in the chaparral, oak woodlands and dry conifer forests surrounding the Sacramento Valley. In southwestern Oregon, it has only a few scattered individuals. It can tolerate extreme heat and harsh soil conditions, but it does not tolerate snow, so it typically grows below

4,000 feet. It is also known as Shasta cypress, and its common name is also spelled MacNab's.

Similar to Baker's cypress. This is a small, shrubby tree (10 to 40 feet tall), often with multiple trunks and broad crowns almost as wide as the tree is tall. It grows in harsh, open conditions on serpentine soils and in the chaparral brushlands. Mature leaves are scale-like, and gray to blue-green growing in opposite pairs; the back side of each leaf has a distinct white resin dot often accompanied by a whitish bloom. Unlike other cypresses, its foliage tends to lie in flattened sprays. Juvenile foliage is narrow and sharply pointed. Its small, round, woody cones are ½ to 1 inch in diameter. Each cone scale typically has a hornlike projection. Cones stay closed on the tree for several years until opened by fire or extreme heat (that is, they are serotinous).

Fire-related species. Fires often kill the tops of the trees, but cause the cones to open, spreading seeds across the landscape. Because of the harsh conditions, very few seedlings mature into trees.

McNab's cypress

Pygmy cypress

Cupressus pigmaea
or *Hesperocyparis pigmaea*

Pygmy or Mendocino cypress? These are different names for the same rare species of cypress native to the north-central California coast. A low elevation species, trees typically grow between 100 to 2,000 feet in elevation. When growing on the nutrient-starved, ancient beach terraces of Mendocino County, they grow in pygmy forests only a few meters tall — hence the name "pygmy." But when growing off these sites, it has been known to approach 8 feet in diameter and 200 feet tall — the largest of all the North American cypresses. As a result of this size difference, some prefer to use the common name "Mendocino." Regardless of the name used, what a difference a site makes!

Pygmy cypress

Even more rare in Oregon. This cypress is even more rare in the Northwest, with only several individuals growing along the southern coast of Oregon. It wasn't even identified there until the 1970s, although several stumps were later discovered that were estimated at 300 to 500 years old — indicating a much longer history in Oregon. In both Oregon and California, it seems to benefit immensely from mild temperatures and summer fogs along the coast.

Identifying clues. Like all cypresses, its mature foliage is scale-like and tightly appressed to the twig; it is light-to-dark green and lacks active resin glands and bloom. Juvenile leaves are more sharply pointed. Cones are small and round (½ to 1 inch in diameter), with three to four pairs of oppositely arranged scales. Scales are nearly smooth with one small prickle on the back of each one. Cones remain closed on the tree until fire dries out the resin that holds the scales closed; this allows the cones to release their seeds following the fire to help recolonize the burned-over site.

Pygmy cypress cones

Sargent's cypress

Cupressus sargentii or *Hesperocyparis sargentii*

Endemic to California coast. This tree is fairly common in the coastal ranges of central and southern California, but it can only be found in several locations in southwestern Oregon. It grows within conifer forests, but also in chaparral brushfields. Like most other cypresses, it competes well on harsh, serpentine soils where other species find it difficult to survive.

Another small conifer. On good sites, it can reach 50 feet tall, but on poor soils and in harsh conditions it grows as stunted, dwarfed trees under 15 feet tall in "pygmy forests." Mature leaves are scale-like, thickened and coarse, with small glands on their backsides, but these glands don't typically produce sticky resin; waxy bloom occurs along the edges of many leaves. This waxy bloom and lack of resin dots helps distinguish it from other Oregon cypresses.

Sargent's cypress

Like other cypresses, juvenile leaves are often sharply pointed. Cones are round, about 1 inch in diameter, and woody with three to four pairs of blistered scales; they often grow on a distinct stalk (called a peduncle).

Fire and soil dependent. Like most of the western cypresses, most of its cones stay on the tree, closed, until opened by fire — but some cones open without fire, so seeds are dispersed more regularly than most other cypresses. And like all of the four Northwestern cypresses, it most often grows on harsh, serpentine sites; in California it may form pure stands on these sites.

PHOTO: U.S. FOREST SERVICE

Douglas-firs fill the view from Bald Knob Lookout in the Rogue River Siskiyou National Forest.

Douglas-firs *Pseudotsuga*

Douglas-fir is the name of an entire genus of trees that contains about six species worldwide — two native to North America and four (or so) native to eastern Asia. Because of its similarity to other genera, Douglas-fir has, through the years, proven difficult to classify. It has, at various times since its discovery, been categorized as a pine, a spruce, a hemlock and a true fir. In 1867, because of its distinctive cones, it was given its own genus — *Pseudotsuga* — which means false hemlock. The hyphen in the common name lets us know that Douglas-fir is not a "true" fir — that it's not a member of the *Abies* genus.

Only one species of Douglas-fir is native to the Northwest, and it's by far the most important member of its entire genus. The other North American Douglas-fir (bigcone Douglas-fir) occupies a very small, scattered range in the coastal mountains of southern California. Its existence in only a few mountain valleys is continually threatened by large wildfires that frequent southern California.

Douglas-fir cone

Douglas-fir *Pseudotsuga menziesii*

The Northwest's most common tree. West of the Cascade crest, you could guess that any conifer in the forest is a Douglas-fir and be right roughly eight out of 10 times. Douglas-fir also is common east of the Cascades, growing at mid to high elevations throughout the Rocky Mountain complex. Douglas-fir is Oregon's state tree.

The cone everybody knows. Put a Douglas-fir cone among all conifer cones of the Northwest and it stands out. Only Douglas-fir has

Douglas-fir

three-pointed bracts sticking out between the cone scales like little tongues. These bracts have been compared to a three-pronged pitchfork and to the hind feet and tail of a mouse diving into its hole. Cones are almost always present, either on the trees or under them. Even trees 6 to 10 years old often bear cones. Note that noble fir also has bracts that are longer than their cone scales, but they are not three-pronged like those of Douglas-fir, and their cones stick up rather than hang down.

Other clues to identification. The buds of Douglas-fir also help identify it. They're sharp-pointed, have reddish-brown overlapping scales, and shine like a highly polished shoe. The needles usually surround the twig like the bristles of a bottle brush and are soft to touch — but when grown in dark shade, they may flatten out. Cut bark reveals two layers of alternating color (red and cream) that look like the ends of sliced bacon. Stands of Douglas-fir are striking from a distance because of the uniform angles of their upper limbs.

Layers of bark resemble the ends of bacon.

A special name. This tree's name reflects the uncertainty that surrounded it for so many years and, at the same time, honors two of the outstanding naturalists of all time. The common name, Douglas-fir, honors the young Scottish botanist David Douglas, who roamed the Northwest in the 1820s while working for the Royal Horticultural Society of England. The *"menziesii"* in the scientific name honors Archibald Menzies, the Scottish physician and naturalist who was the first European to identify this tree on Vancouver Island in 1791 while serving in the British Navy.

Tree of 1,000 uses. Douglas-fir trees are tremendously important to the Pacific Northwest, to North America, and to the world. They furnish more products for human use than any other tree in the world. They can be fashioned into poles and beams hundreds of feet long or can be broken into microscopic fibers for making paper. Lumber and plywood from Douglas-fir are used to build houses, farms, factories, bridges, docks, furniture and boats. Resin from its bark is used to make glue and photographic supplies. Shredded bark is a popular mulch under trees and shrubs in home landscapes. Douglas-fir forests

SIZE: Full-grown trees commonly exceed 250' in height and 10' in diameter. In 2019, the world's tallest Douglas-fir grew in Coos County, Oregon, exceeding 327' tall and over 11' in diameter (and still growing).

NEEDLES: About 1" long with a blunt tip. Spirally arranged around the twig but may be two-ranked in the shade. Green above with two white stomatal bands underneath.

FRUIT: Woody cone 3–4" long; pitchfork-shaped bracts are longer than scales. Hang down.

TWIGS: Large, pointed buds with reddish-brown, overlapping scales. Small, round, partially raised leaf scars.

BARK: Has resin blisters when young; deeply furrowed and reddish-brown when mature.

are home to a wide array of wildlife: elk, bobcats, cougars, bears and deer; and a tremendous variety of birds, insects and small mammals. The soil in Douglas-fir forests is rich in nutrients and soil organisms, and plays a vital role in filtering our water supply. Douglas-fir forests are also among the nation's most heavily used for recreation, and Douglas-fir is the nation's most popular Christmas tree.

Fire — friend and foe. Fire is both a friend and foe to Douglas-fir, depending on the size of the trees and the size of the fire. Large Douglas-firs have very thick bark that can resist the heat of all but the hottest fires. Therefore, in an older forest, small fires simply clear competing vegetation from around larger Douglas-firs. Because Douglas-fir seeds need to germinate on bare mineral soil, they often seed-in after fires that consume the needles, branches, and green plants that typically occupy the forest floor. Large, catastrophic fires, however, kill trees both large and small. Many of the vast stands of old-growth Douglas-fir that currently occupy western Oregon and Washington owe their existence to huge fires that swept through the Northwest 400 to 600 years ago.

Large, old Douglas-firs

Eastside Douglas-fir. East of the Cascade summit, Douglas-fir is a smaller tree than its westside counterparts, although it is still among the largest trees in eastside forests. Its cones are shorter and have stiffer bracts. This eastside variety is commonly called Rocky Mountain Douglas-fir (*P. menziesii* var. *glauca)*, and it ranges from Canada to Mexico.

False cedars

Thuja, Calocedrus, Chamaecyparis, Callitropsis

Common names can be confusing — and that is certainly the case with the false cedars. The Northwest has four species of trees that are called "cedars," but none of them is truly a cedar. In fact, they don't even resemble true cedars. True cedars belong to the genus *Cedrus* (a member of the pine family) and bear their evergreen needles in dense clusters on small, woody spur shoots. Their cones are large, sit upright on their branches (resembling small barrels), and fall apart when the seeds are ripe. True cedars are native only to the Mediterranean and Himalayan regions of the world.

The Northwest's false cedars have tiny, scale-like foliage and small cones that remain on the tree long after their seeds are gone. Why then are they called "cedars"? Although we can't be sure, it's probably because of their wood. In ancient Rome, *Cedrus* referred to a group of trees with fragrant wood. Our "cedars" also have aromatic wood, and that's probably how the confusion in names first started.

Cones of Port-Orford-cedar, a false cedar

It's easy to recognize our false cedars as a group, but it's much more difficult to tell one from another. Their tiny, scale-like leaves overlap like shingles and form flat sprays like many ferns. Some have

Western redcedar, a false cedar　　　　Deodar cedar, a true cedar

distinctive patterns of white bloom on their undersides, others don't. To make things even more complex, the four separate species fall into four different genera. Cones are often the best way to tell them apart.

All false cedars have scale-like foliage, although each differs slightly in shape, and some differ in bloom pattern. Using cones together with leaves aids identification. The Northwest's four species fall into four separate genera, which is confusing to many.

- **Alaska-cedar** was once considered a *Chamaecyparis*, but is now classified as a *Callitropsis*; some even consider it a *Cupressus*. Its needles and cones both resemble those of the genus *Chamaecyparis*, but its ancestry is a bit different.

- **Incense-cedar** is considered a *Calocedrus*, which is called the incense-cedar genus. Because there is only one North American species in this genus, we also call the species incense-cedar. All incense-cedars have cones shaped like a duck's bill when closed and a flying goose when open; this is their best identifying characteristic.

- **Port-Orford-cedar** is considered a *Chamaecyparis*, which is commonly called the white-cedar or false cypress genus (but it is neither a cedar nor a cypress, which is all the more confusing). All members of this genus have small, round, woody cones.

- **Western redcedar** is considered a *Thuja*, which is called the arborvitae genus (there is no genus actually called "redcedar"). All arborvitae have cones shaped like the bowl of a smoker's pipe or a tiny rosebud. In Europe, and much of the world, our western redcedar is called giant arborvitae, because it is the largest member of the arborvitae genus.

If you're confused by all of this, don't worry — I think many of us are!

Alaska-cedar or Alaska-yellow-cedar

Callitropsis nootkatensis • Formerly *Chamaecyparis nootkatensis*

Identity crisis. This tree was first classified in the mid-1800s as *Chamaecyparis nootkatensis*. That made sense because it looks so much like other members of the Chamaecyparis genus. More recently, it has been classified as *Callitropsis*, or even, by some, as *Cupressus*, based on chemical and genetic analyses. Of course, it's still the same tree, and IT doesn't really care what it's called. So, at least for the time being, we'll go with the current majority and use *Callitropsis*. But don't be surprised

Characteristic drooping foliage of Alaska-cedar

to see it change in the future, as its heritage gets sorted out. Perhaps you can avoid confusion by using its common name, Alaska-cedar or Alaska-yellow-cedar, because its wood turns sulfur-yellow when wet; but it is also called Nootka-cypress or Nootka-cedar by some.

Similar to Port-Orford-cedar. Alaska-cedar and Port-Orford-cedar look a lot alike, but there are several ways to tell them apart. Unlike Port-Orford-cedar, there are usually no white X's on the underside of Alaska-cedar needles. Also, they grow in very different habitats. In the Pacific Northwest, Alaska-cedar grows only in cold, wet spots near tree line in the High Cascades, and almost always north of Mount Jefferson, Oregon; while Port-Orford-cedar hugs the coast in southern Oregon and northwestern California. Both species have small, round cones,

Alaska-cedar foliage

but the scales of Port-Orford-cedar cones are wrinkled, while those of Alaska-cedar are smooth except for a pointed projection on the back of each scale. Long, drooping sprays give Alaska-cedar a pronounced weeping appearance and cause many people to think that the tree is sick or dying; in fact, this droopiness is important in shedding heavy, wet snow. When wet, its wood is said to

SIZE: Can grow to 100' tall and 4' in diameter, but usually is smaller.

NEEDLES: Scale-like and appressed to twig, but with flaring tips. Usually no white pattern on underside.

FRUIT: Small, round, woody cones similar to Port-Orford-cedar, but with smooth scales topped with small points.

BARK: Gray and stringy; often pulling away from tree.

FORM: Droopy, weeping appearance.

Alaska-cedar bark

Cones

smell like a moldy potato; it also snaps and pops when burned because of internal moisture, so don't sleep too close to a campfire burning Alaska-cedar. The scientific name *nootkatensis* commemorates the place it was first seen by Europeans, Nootka Sound on Vancouver Island.

Uses. The wood of Alaska-cedar is very resistant to insects and decay and is of good commercial quality, but the tree is so scarce in Oregon and Washington that it has little commercial value here. However, in Canada and coastal Alaska, it's very valuable. The sweet-smelling wood is very durable, is easily worked, and can be finished beautifully. It's especially attractive in window frames and exterior doors and finds many uses in boat construction. Indigenous people of southeast Alaska carved canoe paddles and ceremonial masks from this wood. Like Port-Orford-cedar, Alaska-cedar often is exported to Japan as a substitute for Hinoki cypress. Alaska-cedar also is prized for ornamental purposes because of its beautiful weeping growth form.

Incense-cedar

Calocedrus decurrens formerly *Libocedrus decurrens*

A false cedar. Like the other false cedars, incense-cedar has scale-like leaves. However, when taken together, each set of four leaves is much longer than it is wide. (Other false cedars have sets of four leaves about as wide as they are long.) Many say a set of four small scales resembles a long-stemmed wine glass. The cones of incense-cedar are also much different from those of other "cedars" — when open, they look like a flying goose or Donald Duck's bill with his tongue sticking out. The hyphen in the common name reminds us that this is not a true cedar.

Incense-cedar

Incense-cedar foliage

Rumpled appearance. Branches of mature incense-cedars have a twisted, rumpled appearance, while young trees growing in the open form perfect pyramids. John Muir, one of America's most famous early naturalists, observed that the dense, matted foliage of vigorously growing incense-cedars made a fine shelter from storms. Incense-cedar is a good ornamental or windbreak tree, especially in drier parts of Oregon, although it is not native to Washington. It's fast growing, attractive and reasonably free of insects and diseases. However, near the edges of its natural range it appears to be suffering from climates that are warmer and drier than in the past; this results in yellowing foliage that dies and falls prematurely from the tree.

SIZE: Grows to 110' tall and 5' in diameter.

NEEDLES: Scale-like and appressed to twig; set of four leaves is much longer than it is wide and is shaped like a long-stemmed wine glass; usually with little or no white bloom on underside.

FRUIT: Woody cones about 1" long; unopened cones are shaped like a duck's bill; open cones are shaped like a flying goose.

BARK: Flaky when young; platy, furrowed and reddish brown when mature.

Brown female cones and yellow pollen cones

Pencil wood. Incense-cedar has aromatic wood that resists insects and decay. However, much wood that otherwise would make quality lumber is riddled by a white fungus called "pencil rot" or "peck." As a result, it seldom finds its way into decking, siding, or shingles. However, its wood is soft, pliable and easy to machine without splintering — properties that make it one of the few woods in the world suitable for making wooden pencils. In fact, most of the world's supply of wooden pencils once came from southern Oregon. Although incense-cedars are not often used for Christmas trees, the yellow pollen cones that develop midwinter make the branches popular for wreaths and swags.

Where it grows. Incense-cedar grows throughout most of the Oregon Cascades but is not native north of the Oregon-Washington border. It becomes increasingly common south of Santiam Pass in Oregon. It is a principal tree in California's forests because it is well adapted to droughty conditions and extreme temperatures (both hot and cold).

Port-Orford-cedar *Chamaecyparis lawsoniana*

Another false cedar. Port-Orford-cedar looks a lot like western redcedar — except that Port-Orford-cedar has round cones rather than rosebud-shaped cones, and Port-Orford-cedar has white X's, rather than butterflies, underneath its needles. Again, the hyphens in the name tell us that this is not a true cedar.

Port-Orford-cedar

Small range. Port-Orford-cedar's native range is very small — a coastal belt stretching 200 miles south from Coos Bay, Oregon to Arcata, California, and less than 50 miles inland. In spite of this, it's a familiar tree throughout cooler, wetter portions of the Northwest where so many have been planted either as ornamentals for their beautiful shape or for windbreaks because of their uniform growth and dense foliage. Nurseries often incorrectly call Port-Orford-cedars "cypresses." Many ornamental varieties have been developed from the forest species.

Health concerns. In the mid-1900s, a non-native root rot known as *Phytophthora lateralis* became a serious killer of Port-Orford-cedar throughout its range. *Phytophthora* is a waterborne pathogen and

SIZE: Grows to 200' tall and 6' in diameter.

NEEDLES: scale-like and appressed to the twig. Undersides bear distinct white "X."

FRUIT: Small, round, woody cones about ¼–½" in diameter. Young cones are green to blue, but turn brown with age.

BARK: Brown, fibrous and ridged. Thicker than the bark of other false cedars.

under normal conditions spreads slowly (and downhill). However, it's also picked up by car and truck tires and is spread rapidly (and often uphill) by logging trucks and recreational vehicles. Few trees that lie in its path escape alive. Nevertheless, Port-Orford-cedar is so beautiful that many people still risk planting it. If you decide to plant it, select a site where the soil is well drained and won't be disturbed. Disease-resistant varieties are also becoming more available. Port-Orford-cedar planted outside its native range is also susceptible to droughts, insects and disease as our climate becomes warmer and drier.

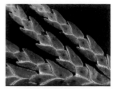

Note the white "x" between the leaves.

Valuable wood. Years ago, the Japanese fell in love with the wood of Port-Orford-cedar because its light color and straight grain reminded them of their sacred Hinoki cypress, a member of the same genus as Port-Orford-cedar (*Chamaecyparis*). Their heavy buying of Port-Orford-cedar and the small supply of trees make good logs very high in price. The wood of Port-Orford-cedar is durable, easy to work, aromatic and pleasingly textured. Locally, it's used similarly to western redcedar. Archers once used it for arrow shafts, but they now rely mostly on fiberglass and aluminum alloys. Boughs are very popular in wreaths and floral displays because of their soft blue foliage and interesting round cones; as a result they are commonly are shipped around the world for this purpose.

Blue maturing cones and brown mature cones

The future. While Port-Orford-cedar's future is uncertain because of Phytophthera and a climate that is getting warmer and drier, scientists have been actively exploring solutions. Strains of Port-Orford-cedar that are resistant to *Phytophthera* are now available and entering the marketplace.

Western redcedar *Thuja plicata*

To know western redcedar. Cones and foliage both provide good clues for identifying western redcedar. This is the only native "cedar" that has cones turned up and bent backward on the branch. Before opening, they look like the bowl of a smoker's pipe; after opening, they look a bit like tiny rose buds. If you look closely at the underside of the foliage and use your imagination, you can often see a tiny butterfly (some would say bowtie) outlined in white. The growth form of western redcedar is also a good clue to its identity. The dense, frondlike branches look as if they could shed rain; in fact, some Northwest Indians had a name for this tree which means "dry underneath."

Western redcedar female cones

The name game. The genus name, *Thuja*, comes from an ancient Greek word for a highly prized aromatic wood. The species name, *plicata*, means folded into plaits (interwoven); it was probably suggested by the flattened twigs and the fine, regular arrangement of the scale-like

Western redcedar

leaves. Or, it could come from the long, stringy bark from which fibrous strips are easily pulled. The common name, redcedar, refers to the red heartwood so common in older trees. Redcedar is written as one word (or, less commonly, hyphenated) to indicate that it's not a true cedar.

Where it grows. Western redcedar grows along the Northwest coast, from Alaska to northern California and from the Pacific Ocean to Montana (skipping over the too-arid parts of central and eastern Oregon and Washington). It typically grows in moist habitats but sometimes is found on drier mountain slopes. Its commercial range is really the coastal fog belt; because they are so damp, western Washington and Canada have far greater numbers of these trees than Oregon. The swollen bases of western redcedar make it the broadest of northwest trees — sometimes surpassing 20 feet in diameter!

SIZE: Grow to 200' tall and 10' or more in diameter. Often have swollen, fluted trunks.

NEEDLES: Scale-like and appressed to twig. Green above but with a white butterfly pattern below.

FRUIT: Small woody cones about 1/2" long; grow upright on twig. Shaped like tiny rose buds or the bowl of a smoker's pipe.

BARK: Thin, reddish-brown and stringy.

What it's used for. One of the lightest of coniferous woods, western redcedar is soft in texture, even- and straight-grained, highly attractive, and pleasant to smell. Since the heartwood resists decay, it's prized for uses where it will be exposed to the weather. Unfortunately, old-growth trees that made redcedar's reputation are becoming scarce, and the upcoming second growth is less resistant to insects and decay. Nevertheless, forest managers welcome the persistent natural regeneration that assures future supplies of this legendary species. Always the leader in shingles and siding, redcedar has other important uses such as poles, posts, pilings, fencing, greenhouse equipment, boats, and outdoor decks.

Redcedar and salmon — mainstays of Northwest Indians. In days gone by, salmon crowding Northwest rivers assured freedom from hunger, while western redcedar, growing conveniently nearby, supplied material for building lodges and boats, tools and utensils, and a hundred other uses. Strips of bark were fashioned into clothes, baskets, ropes, and fishing nets. For each Northwest Indian relic of stone that we find, there once were innumerable articles of wood and bark.

Northwest Indian transportation. Northwest Indians made redcedar canoes by the thousands. They would fell a single tree, cut it to the desired length, and hollow it out, using a combination of fire and tools made from stone and animal bone. Next, it was filled with water into which hot stones were dropped, causing the water to boil and soften the wood so the sides could be spread and curved to the proper form. Abrasive stones that the Indians used to smooth the sides of canoes (and other wood articles) are still found at old dwelling sites. Around

The underside of western redcedar foliage shows a "butterfly" or "bowtie" pattern.

1900, Captain J.C. Voss purchased an ordinary 38-foot dugout cedar canoe from Indigenous people on Vancouver Island. Adding a cabin and three small masts, he sailed it 40,000 miles to circumnavigate the globe. This canoe is now housed in Thunderbird Park, Victoria.

The fiber of life. Northwest Indians and Indigenous people of Canada used the inner bark of western redcedar to make blankets, skirts, nets, ropes, mats, baskets, shawls and other necessities of home and livelihood. Easily worked, redcedar wood was a favorite for implements such as arrow and spear shafts, bowls, spoons and handles, as well as for toys and artwork. Bark fibers twisted into ropes were used to lash house timbers together, taking the place of nails. North of Puget Sound, along the coast and its many islands, Northwest Indian craftsmen carved striking designs on redcedar totem poles. Ravens, thunderbirds, bears, wolves, frogs, beavers, salmon and other animals were often carved in humanlike forms to help explain the intricate relationships between humans and the world around them.

Hemlocks *Tsuga*

Hemlocks are noted for short needles and droopy tops (leaders) and branches. There are only about 10 species of hemlock in the world, mostly in North America, China and Japan. The Northwest has two native hemlocks: the abundant and commercially important western hemlock and the lesser known, higher elevation mountain hemlock. Even when found growing together, they're relatively easy to tell apart.

- **Mountain hemlock needles** are blue-green on all surfaces, similar in length and uniformly arranged around the twig. Their cross-section is squarish. Clusters of needles often have a starlike appearance as they radiate away from the twig. Cones are cylindrical and are 1 to 3 inches long.

- **Western hemlock needles** are all very short, but have two distinctly different sizes on the same twig (typically in an alternating pattern). They are yellow-green on top and have two white bands on their undersides. They are flat in cross-section. They tend to stick out the sides of the twigs (appearing to be somewhat two-ranked) but also arise from the top of the twig. Cones are egg-shaped and about 1 inch long.

Western hemlock's characteristic floppy leader

Mountain hemlock *Tsuga mertensiana*

Elevation is the key. In Northwest forests, mountain hemlock is always found near tree line, braving the fury of mountain storms. Farther north in its range, it drops in elevation due to the colder, moister climate. Generally, it grows above the range of western hemlock, but sometimes they intermix. Northwest forests have a considerable number of mountain hemlock, always in high, remote locations. Mountain hemlock ranges from southeast Alaska to central California and eastward into the northern Rockies.

Mountain hemlock

Star-spangled tree. Perhaps the most distinctive feature of mountain hemlock is clusters of needles with a starlike look as they shoot away from the twigs that bear them. Although individual needles are similar to those of many other conifers, most needles of mountain hemlock grow on short shoots and stick out from all sides, giving the appearance of thousands of stars on each branch. Its short needles (under 1 inch long) tend to have a blue-green color (bloom) that makes them highly prized as ornamentals (though this bloom weathers away on older needles). Cones are generally 1 to 3 inches long and have thin, smooth scales. The top branch of the tree and all the lateral branch tips are bent, almost appearing to be broken, but they are not as droopy as those of western hemlock.

Mountain hemlock cones

Uses. When they reach sufficient size, mountain hemlocks are sometimes harvested for pulp and lumber, but their growth is often too slow to be profitable. Many groves are set aside in parks and wilderness areas for their beauty and their value to high-elevation wildlife.

SIZE: Grows to 100' tall and 3' in diameter.

NEEDLES: Under 1" long; all are similar in length; blue-green, especially on young needles; star-like appearance as needles radiate away from short shoots on the branches.

FRUIT: Woody cones 1–3" long; thin, rounded scales.

TWIGS: Moderately stout; many short lateral shoots; terminal branch tips are bent like a limp wrist.

BARK: Reddish-brown with narrow ridges, weathering gray with age; about 1" thick.

Star-like needles of mountain hemlock

Western hemlock *Tsuga heterophylla*

Droopy top and bobbing branches. Mother Nature put a waving banner at the very top of western hemlock, making it easy to identify. The leader, or highest vertical branch, droops over like a buggy whip. Other trees that resemble hemlock — true firs, spruces and Douglas-fir — have stiff, erect leaders. False cedars also have drooping leaders, but their flat sprays of scale-like leaves are unlike hemlock.

Western hemlock

Unique needles. Notice the short needles that pop out on top of the twigs. The other needles are usually in ranks like soldiers, but not those short ones — they are in disarray. Western hemlock needles are thin, flat, and blunt — almost as blunt as the end of your finger. They differ noticeably in length but average less than ½ inch — the shortest needles of any conifer in this region. Hemlock cones also are very small — usually less than 1 inch long — and when open, they're egg-shaped. Individual trees often bear tremendous numbers of cones.

Changing importance. As late as 1930, lumbermen did not want western hemlock. But times have changed. No tree exceeds this one in pulp quality and yield for high-quality newsprint and book, magazine and tissue papers. It's also used for plywood and some solid wood products. Gym floors are often made of hemlock because it resists mechanical abrasion better than other softwoods and becomes harder with age.

Hemlock ecology. Western hemlock can thrive in heavy shade. Seedlings can fight through thick patches of competing vegetation to form dense, multilayered "climax forests," in which young hemlocks grow under older hemlocks and Douglas-firs. Its tolerance to shade also enables trees to grow close together. As a result, forests that include western hemlock grow more wood per acre than any other forest, except possibly the remarkable redwoods. The thin bark of western hemlock makes it vulnerable to attacks from insect and diseases, and its shallow roots put it at risk to windthrow. Hemlocks shower incredible numbers of far-flying seeds, so tiny that a pound might contain 300,000 of them! The seeds sprout easily and are often found on rotting stumps and mossy logs (often called "nurse logs" because they nurture so many seedlings).

SIZE: Grows to 200' tall and 4' in diameter.

NEEDLES: Short (under ¾" long); several distinct sizes; green above with white bands underneath each needle; most needles appear to arise from the sides of the twigs but a few are arrayed along the top of each twig.

FRUIT: Small, woody cones (about 1"); egg-shaped; thin, smooth scales.

TWIGS: Thin and droopy; leaf scars are partially raised pegs.

BARK: Thin (under 1"); flattened ridges; inner bark is reddish with purple streaks.

Western hemlock needles have two different lengths.

Western hemlock cones of different ages

Loves cool, cloudy conditions. The more rain and fog, the more western hemlock seems at home. This tree with its graceful feathery limbs is a good rainfall indicator. At 60 inches of rain per year, it masses in dense, dark forests of the Coast and Cascade ranges; below 60 inches, it becomes scarce. Western hemlock stretches from southeastern Alaska to northern California and eastward into the northern Rockies, skipping over the drier areas of central and eastern Oregon and Washington. Western hemlock is Washington's state tree.

Junipers *Juniperus*

Junipers are strange conifers indeed. The fruits of most junipers typically look like blue berries (although immature fruits are green and some mature berries may be red, tan or copper). In fact, their fruits are round cones, but they're more leathery than the typical woody cones of conifers. Junipers typically (but not always) bear male and female flowers on separate trees, so only female trees have fruit. Juniper foliage may be scale-like, needle-like, or both, and it often has a distinctive fragrance that carries quite a distance.

California juniper

Three junipers (western, Rocky Mountain, and common) are clearly native to Oregon, while opinions differ about whether California juniper is slowly moving into the chaparral regions of southern Oregon. Western juniper is perhaps the most common, although in central and eastern Oregon and Washington you're also likely to encounter Rocky Mountain juniper. Common juniper, which is always shrub-like rather than treelike, commonly occurs in alpine situations. Northwest junipers do not typically grow together, making the identification challenge a bit easier.

Common juniper

- **California juniper's** foliage is similar to western and Rocky Mountain juniper. Mature cones are reddish brown (rather than blue) and grow on short stalks. Because of its uncertain status in Oregon and Washington, it won't be described further in this book.

- **Common juniper** grows primarily at high elevations. It always has a shrub-like or matted growth form with individual, needle-like leaves about ½ inch long (no scale-like leaves). It grows only as a shrub in Oregon, so it won't be described further in this book.

Rocky Mountain juniper

- **Rocky Mountain juniper** resembles western juniper, except that its needles do not have resin dots. It grows primarily along the Idaho border in Oregon, but is more widespread in central and eastern Washington and southern British Columbia.

- **Western juniper** has both scale-like and needle-like leaves, each with a sticky, aromatic dot of resin on it (clear and sticky when fresh, and white and less sticky as it ages). It has an upright growth form and grows on hot, dry, low-elevation sites in Central and eastern Oregon and southeastern Washington. Needle-like leaves are very short and sharp, and are commonly referred to as "awl-like."

Western juniper

Rocky Mountain juniper *Juniperus scopulorum*

Widespread juniper. Although it occurs sporadically in eastern Washington and Oregon, it is widespread throughout the sprawling Rocky Mountain complex from central British Columbia to our border with Mexico. The species epithet — *scopulorum* — means "of the mountains."

Similar to western juniper. Most junipers look alike. Like many junipers, the leaves of Rocky Mountain juniper are awl-like when young and scale-like when mature. They seldom overlap on the same-aged twig, and they don't usually contain white, sticky resin dots. Like all junipers, the fruits of Rocky Mountain junipers are berrylike. They are blue or tan when young and dark blue to almost black when mature (darker than other junipers), though they're often covered in a white bloom.

Where it grows. Rocky Mountain juniper prefers dry areas — open forests, open brushlands, and even grasslands. It is not tolerant of shade. In the absence of fire, they are long-lived, up to 300 years (though the Jardine Juniper near Logan, Utah may exceed 1,500 years). Like all junipers, the seeds are wingless and so don't fly — instead, they rely on animals for dispersal.

Hybridizes with eastern redcedar. When Rocky Mountain juniper meets eastern redcedar (*Juniperus virginiana*) along the east flank of the Rockies, they sometimes hybridize.

Healing powers. Indigenous people commonly consider the smoke of burning juniper to have healing powers.

Juniper of Puget Sound. There's a juniper unique to the Puget Sound area that some consider a variety of Rocky Mountain juniper and some consider a separate species (*Juniperus maritima,* seaside juniper). Its characteristics are nearly identical to Rocky Mountain juniper, but chemical and DNA analyses suggest that it might merit its own species designation.

SIZE: Can reach 30' tall and 1–2' in diameter, but most often smaller. Commonly has short, multiple-branched trunk.

NEEDLES: Leaves are primarily opposite, but sometimes in whorls of three. Juvenile leaves are awl-like and older leaves are scale-like, seldom overlapping on the same twig. The back of each needle has a raised gland that is not usually resinous. Less fragrant than western juniper.

FRUIT: Small, round "berry" (actually a nonwoody cone) that is light blue or tan when immature but dark blue to almost black when mature; typically covered in white bloom. Male and female "flowers" are typically borne on separate plants.

BARK: Thin, reddish-brown, and fibrous.

Rocky Mountain juniper

Western juniper *Juniperus occidentalis*

Distinctive tree. Western juniper is known by almost everyone who lives in eastern Oregon and Washington. Western junipers are small evergreen trees with thin, shreddy bark, bluish "berries," and tiny, scale-like needles that are scratchy to the touch. Each scale has a small gland on its back where there is a tiny drop of resin that seals the breathing pore to conserve moisture. The resin exuded from these glands is clear when young but turns white with age. It is always sticky and aromatic — a good identifying characteristic.

A western juniper from the Oregon-Idaho border

SIZE: Can reach 60′ tall and 3′ in diameter, but most often smaller. Commonly has short, multiple-branched trunk.

NEEDLES: Combination of scale-like and awl-like needles; back of each needle has a clear or white resin dot. Distinctive fragrance.

FRUIT: Small, round, blue "berry" (actually a nonwoody cone).

BARK: Thin, reddish-brown and fibrous.

About those berries. Juniper "berries" are really cones with tough, fleshy scales that seldom open. Usually, they must get digested by a bird in order to germinate. They take two years to mature and typically have a bluish-white coating (called bloom) that can be rubbed off. The resin inside these "berries" has a strong, distinctive odor of its own. In Central and eastern Oregon and Washington, "home on the range" means the scent of western juniper and sagebrush.

The camel of trees. As you emerge from mountainous forests of the Cascades into Central Oregon and Washington, you enter an open juniper woodland. Western juniper grows throughout the arid West but seems to find a special home in Central Oregon. Western juniper is the "camel" of our trees, living on less water in dry climates than any other Northwest tree. Where it has moisture, western juniper will grow more than 50 feet tall, but typically it's shorter. Although it usually grows alone, it may be joined by ponderosa pine if rainfall is above 12 inches.

Berrylike cones of western juniper

Resin dots on the foliage of western juniper

Expanding range. The range of western juniper has expanded rapidly since white settlement, which brought with it fire suppression. While some view this as a good thing, others realize that junipers remove much more water from the ecosystem than do native grasses and shrubs. As a result, many are calling for the reduction of western juniper, back to its historic range.

More about juniper. Despite their short stature, western junipers commonly live to be several hundred years old. In the great juniper groves of central Oregon, some grow to be 4 to 5 feet thick. Half-dead, gnarled, and ghostlike, they tell of a tenacious struggle to survive where no other tree can. Ogden Wayside near Terrebonne, Oregon has a sample of these ancient and craggy junipers, a different but memorable forest. The scientific name, *occidentalis*, means western, referring to the fact that it grows in western North America.

Uses. The wood of western juniper is used locally for fuel, fence posts, and gift shop novelties. Fence posts made of durable juniper heartwood are said to outlast two post holes. Northwest Indians traditionally eat the berries. Deer and cattle browse the foliage, and birds and small animals feast on the berries. Juniper cones are also used as a cooking spice, especially in Europe, and to flavor the alcoholic beverage, gin.

Larches *Larix*

Larches are different from most conifers because they're deciduous — they lose their needles in the fall. Also, their needles are arranged differently from those of most conifers. On current-year twigs they're borne singly, but on older twigs they arise in dense clusters from stout, woody pegs that resemble wooden barrels. Only about 10 species of larch grow in the world, mostly in cold and snowy parts of the northern hemisphere. Only western larch is native to Oregon, but subalpine larch grows in Washington, Idaho and southern British Columbia. Larches are sometimes called tamaracks, especially by people whose roots are in eastern North America.

Subalpine larch
fall foliage
glows in the
Alpine Lakes
Wilderness Area
of Washington.

PHOTO: U.S. FOREST SERVICE

Subalpine larch *Larix lyallii*

A high elevation, eastside species. Subalpine larch typically grows east of the Cascade crest at high elevations in Washington and in the northern Rockies of Idaho, Alberta and

Subalpine larch fall foliage

British Columbia. Especially magnificent stands grow in and around Banff National Park of Alberta, Canada. It does not occur in Oregon. It typically grows on shallow, rocky soils near tree line. It may grow in pure stands or mixed with other high elevation conifers, such as subalpine fir and whitebark pine.

Its value is not monetary. Because of its small stature and very limited range, subalpine larch has no commercial value for wood products. However, many timberline birds and mammals feed within its stands. Its needles are a primary food source for blue grouse, and woodpeckers and other cavity nesters depend on it for nesting sites. Stands of subalpine larch are a truly magnificent site in the fall when they turn brilliant yellow. But be quick when you want to photograph them, because the color often lasts only a few days.

Why deciduous? Shedding their leaves in winter helps subalpine larch to avoid water stress and to survive in their harsh winter environment.

Old age. Even though they live in a harsh environment, subalpine larches can often reach 400 to 500 years old, and sometimes 1,000 years or more.

Western larch *Larix occidentalis*

Yellow in fall, naked in winter. In the fall of the year, western larch is as easy to recognize as an apple tree. Its needles turn bright yellow and drop to the ground. After standing bare all winter, larch dons new spring clothes of light green. Of the western conifers, only subalpine larch is similarly bright yellow in the fall and bright green in the spring.

Identifying western larch. Western and subalpine larches are the only Northwestern conifers that shed their needles in winter (although dawn redwood and baldcypress are common ornamentals that are also deciduous). This alone makes them easy to identify in our forests. Other features that help identify western larch include needles

Western larch cones

SIZE: Typically 40–50' tall and 1–2' in diameter, but the record tree reached 95' tall and over 6' in diameter.

NEEDLES: Deciduous (fall from the tree in winter); borne on woody pegs in clusters of 30–40 (more than western larch); 1–2" long; bluish-green and squarish in cross-section. Young shoots are often covered in dense, woolly white hairs.

FRUIT: Small, woody cones (1–2" long); papery bracts are longer than scales. Reddish brown when mature. Edges of scales are irregularly toothed.

TWIGS: Have conspicuous pegs from which needles arise.

BARK: Mature bark is thin, furrowed and flakes off in irregular-shaped pieces. Reddish to purplish brown.

A stand of western larch

that are clustered on stout, woody pegs, and "whiskery" cones, with bracts longer than the cone scales. Old larches have colorful reddish bark that flakes off in jigsaw puzzle pieces (similar to ponderosa pine, only redder). The trunk of western larch is straight as a flagpole, and the crown is so open you can see the entire trunk and all its short, horizontal branches. Western larch is a large, fast-growing tree for the dry forests it occupies. It's long-lived, often exceeding 500 years.

Where it grows. In the Pacific Northwest, look for western larch in eastside mountain ranges between 2,000 and 7,000 feet. Although these forests are dry by westside standards, western larch prefers comparatively moist locations such as north-facing slopes and valley bottoms. Common associates are Douglas-fir and ponderosa pine on drier sites, and subalpine fir and Engelmann spruce on cooler, wetter sites.

Uses. Western larch produces lumber that is well-liked for general construction. Higher grades have an attractive grain and are used for interior finish. It's also valuable for posts, poles and mine timbers because of its resistance to decay, and it is commonly used to build log cabins because of its straightness and small amount of taper from end-to-end. A heavy wood, larch firewood produces a great deal of heat.

Response to fire. The thick bark of mature western larches makes them reasonably resistant to fire, as does the fact that the foliage is intolerant of shade, so lower limbs typically drop from the tree as it ages. Its seeds are good at colonizing the open, burned-over spaces following fire. Healthy larch stands depend on periodic fire to maintain their vigor.

SIZE: Grows to 180' tall and 4' in diameter.

NEEDLES: Deciduous (fall from the tree in winter); borne singly on first year's twigs, but borne on woody pegs in clusters of 15–30 on older branches (fewer than subalpine larch); 1–2" long; yellow-green

FRUIT: Small, woody cones (1–2" long); papery bracts are longer than scales.

TWIGS: Have short, thick but conspicuous pegs from which needles arise.

BARK: Mature bark is furrowed and flakes off in irregular-shaped pieces. Reddish-orange.

Western larch bark

Pines *Pinus*

Worldwide, pines are the most common type of conifer: there are nearly 100 different species. North America alone has more than 30. In general, pines are easy to distinguish from other needle-leaved trees because:

- **Pines have long, narrow needles bound in bundles** of two to five resembling whisk brooms. (In fact, some whisk brooms are made of pine needles!)

- **Pines have hard, woody cones with thick, tough scales.** Typically, they are egg-shaped.

- **Pine branches usually grow in distinctive "whorls"** or rings around the trunk. Each whorl represents one year's growth. This makes their trunks easy to climb, and makes it easy to estimate how old each tree is.

Pine forests are also distinctive. In general, pine trees like a lot of light, so pine forests are open, with sunlight spilling through to the forest floor. Wind moving through their long needles also gives pine forests a distinctive sound, and no one can miss their unique fragrance.

Eleven species of pine (and several varieties) are native to Oregon and Washington, although many others have been introduced for ornamental reasons. Four of our pines (lodgepole, sugar, ponderosa and western white) were named by Scottish botanist David Douglas. Apparently, this diversity surprised even him, for he wrote to his employer at the Royal Horticultural Society of England, "You will begin to think that I manufacture pines at my pleasure."

To identify pines, first count the needles in each bundle. This will divide the species into smaller groups of two-, three-, and five-needled pines. Then check the appearance of the cones and other needle characteristics like length and color to pinpoint the species. If you're still stuck, check the geographic area in which you've found the pine (assuming that you're out in the forest).

Ponderosa pines dominate the lower elevations leading to The Three Sisters of the Deschutes National Forest in Central Oregon.

Frost coats the long, narrow needles of a ponderosa pine in the Wallowa-Whitman National Forest.

PHOTO: U.S. FOREST SERVICE

Bishop pine *Pinus muricata*

Bishop pine needles

Primarily in California. Bishop pine has a small, scattered distribution along the California coast, south into Baja California. It typically grows within 10 miles of the coast, on shallow, poorly drained soils. It also grows in association with various short-statured pygmy forests that occur on sterile soils along the California coast, although it is seldom stunted itself. Only recently has it been seen growing in a few spots along the southern Oregon Coast.

A religious name. The "bishop" in the common name resulted from Europeans first seeing it near the Mission of San Luis Obispo in southern California.

A fire-related species. Its thick bark helps protect it from fires. Its cones commonly remain closed until the heat of fire dries the resin in them and causes them to open, releasing their seeds. Some cones open without fire on very hot California days.

Compared with lodgepole. When compared with lodgepole, bishop pine's needles are longer and straighter, and its cones are larger and heavier.

SIZE: Grows to 75' tall and 2–3' in diameter.

NEEDLES: Two needles per bundle; 3–6" long; commonly straight and stiff.

FRUIT: Egg-shaped but asymmetrical cones, 2–4" long, typically with a stiff prickle at the end of each cone scale. Several often circle the branch. Some cones remain closed on the tree for years, waiting to be opened by the heat of fire; others open on their own.

BARK: Thick, dark gray to black; deeply fissured.

Two-needled pines

BISHOP needles are 3 to 6 inches long, straight, and blue-green to dark green. Cones are 2 to 3½ inches long, egg-shaped but asymmetrical, and armed with a sharp prickle.

LODGEPOLE needles are 1 to 3 inches long, yellow-green to green, and often twist apart. Cones are 1 to 2½ inches long and egg-shaped when open.

A stand of bishop pine; thick, fire-resistant bark; and cones

Lodgepole pine *Pinus contorta*

Commonly called shore pine along the coast
and lodgepole pine in the mountains

Two-needled pine. Lodgepole pine is easy to identify because its
needles occur in two's, are 1 to 3 inches long, and twist apart from one
another, leading to the scientific name *"contorta."* Throughout most
of the Northwest, except for northern California and southwestern
Oregon, it's the only native two-needled pine. Also, its cones and
needles are much smaller than those of our other Northwestern pines.
The prickly, egg-shaped cones are seldom longer than 2 inches, and
may hang on the tree unopened for many years, waiting for the heat of
fire to release their seeds.

SIZE: Grows to 100'
tall and 2' in diameter.
Typically very slender.
Shorter and more
twisted form along the
ocean.

NEEDLES: Two
needles per bundle;
1–3" long; commonly
twist apart from one
another.

FRUIT: Small, egg-
shaped cones (1–2"
long), often with a
prickle at the end of
each cone scale. Some
cones stay closed
on the tree for years,
waiting to be opened
by the heat of fire;
others open on their
own.

BARK: Thin, dark, and
flaky.

Lodgepole pine

Where lodgepole pines grow. Lodgepole pine
is one of the most widely distributed trees in
North America. Two varieties of lodgepole
pine grow in the Northwest — a coastal
form, often called "shore" pine (*P. contorta* var.
contorta), and a mountain form, simply called
"lodgepole" pine (*P. contorta* var. *latifolia*).
Shore pines grow within a few miles of the
coast and are typically bushy and distorted
by the wind — their buds and branches
continually blasted by sand and salt crystals
driven by gale-force winds. Although they're
not particularly important commercially,
they do help stabilize sand dunes, and they
add to the beauty to Northwest coastlines.
The mountain form of lodgepole, on the
other hand, occupies extensive areas at middle and high elevations
throughout western North America and is an important timber tree —
mostly because of its abundance rather than its size or properties. Its
growth form is typically tall, straight and slender, except when growing
near the tree line, where it is often stunted and twisted.

Meaningful name. The mountain lodgepole grows slim and straight
to 80 or even 100 feet. The name seems to have originated with Lewis
and Clark, who noted that American Indians of the Great Plains
traveled to the Rocky Mountains for the slender "lodgepoles" upon
which to raise their lodges or teepees. Such lodgepoles would be used
for a lifetime, until worn out by weathering and handling.

Small tree, large numbers. The western states hold immense supplies
of lodgepole pine. Abundant reproduction causes "dog-hair" thickets
where growth stagnates unless it's thinned, either by wildfire or by
humans. Lodgepole's economic future appears linked to industries
making paper or composition boards for which pine fiber is excellent
and large trees are unnecessary. Currently, the main uses are for
lumber, poles, posts, house logs and fiber products.

**Mature trees
and seedlings of
lodgepole pine**

Fire-related species. With age and overcrowding, lodgepole pine becomes vulnerable to attack from a variety of insects and diseases. Epidemic pine beetle infestations in western North America in the 1970s, 1980s and 1990s have killed many, many trees. Once dead, these dense lodgepole stands are very susceptible to wildfire. Fortunately for lodgepole's survival, it's well prepared: its small, hard cones often stay on the tree unopened until a fire passes through. When the flames die, the cones open, spreading their seeds across the charred ground. As a result, lodgepole seedlings can grow with limited competition from other species.

Lodgepole pines on Santiam Pass, Oregon.

Several varieties. There are four varieties of lodgepole pine. You would recognize them all as *Pinus contorta*, but they each have slightly different characteristics:

- **Bolander beach pine** (*Pinus contorta* var. *bolanderi*) grows only in Mendocino County, along the northwestern California coast.

Shore pines near Florence, Oregon

- **Shore pine** (*Pinus contorta* var. *contorta*) grows along the Pacific coast from southern Alaska to northern California.

- **Lodgepole or Rocky Mountain lodgepole pine** (*Pinus contorta* var. *latifolia*) grows extensively from the Yukon throughout the Rocky Mountains into southern Colorado.

- **Sierra lodgepole pine** (*Pinus contorta* var. *murrayana*) grows throughout the Cascades of Oregon and Sierra Nevadas of California.

Gray pine *Pinus sabiniana*

Primarily a California species. For the most part, gray pine is found in the dry, forested foothills surrounding the Great Valley of California. Only recently has it been found growing in southwestern Oregon, perhaps because of a warming, drying climate.

Also called ghost pine and foothills pine. Its gray needles are easy to spot, even from a distance — hence, the names "gray" and "ghost." It's also called foothills pine in California because that's where it likes to grow — in the open foothills and mountain slopes

Gray pines in Pinnacles National Park, California

A typical gray pine cone and its characteristic gray foliage

below 4,000 feet and adjoining chaparral brushfields. Once called digger pine, that name is no longer favored in North America because it is viewed as derogatory by California Indians. (That name still shows up in older literature and is still often used internationally.)

Unique cones. Cones are a dead giveaway for gray pine. They are 6 to 14 inches long and egg-shaped to nearly round. Cone scales end in sharp, claw-like hooks that get larger and sharper near the base of the cone. They often weigh 1 to 2 pounds. Cones persist on the tree for several years, regardless of whether they have shed their seeds. These large, interesting cones are a favorite of cone collectors of all ages. Note that a purely Californian species, Coulter pine (not described here), has cones that are similar to, but much larger than, gray pine.

Fire-related species. Gray pine has thick bark that helps protect it from fire. It also tends to shed lower branches, which helps keep fire out of its crown. Its large seeds are quite hearty, which helps them recolonize burned sites. The absence of fire from its native ecosystems helps other conifers overtop the shorter, shade intolerant gray pine, often shading them out of the forest.

Jeffrey pine *Pinus jeffreyi*

Another three-needled pine. Jeffrey pine is another Northwest pine with needles clasped in threes. In fact, Jeffrey's needles are so similar to ponderosa's that the two are difficult to tell apart from needles alone. The best way to tell them apart is by their cones: Jeffrey pine has a thicker and larger cone that resembles an old-fashioned beehive or a pineapple. While Jeffrey's cones can vary in length from 5 to 12 inches, the typical huge oval is hard to mistake. Another difference: the prickles on the ends of Jeffrey's cone scales are curved inward (or J-shaped), while ponderosa's are straight.

Expert observers also seem able to single out Jeffrey pine by subtle differences such as a purplish-white bloom on its new twigs (not seen on ponderosa), a pineapple-like odor, or the bark color of old trees: Jeffrey is reddish-brown and ponderosa is yellowish-brown to orange. Also, Jeffrey holds its needles several years longer than ponderosa, so Jeffrey's branches typically have a bushier look than ponderosa's.

SIZE: commonly 30–60' tall and up to 4' in diameter. Although it commonly has only a single trunk, it often has multiple leaders and unruly branches.

NEEDLES: Clusters of three; 8–12" long; distinctly gray-green. Sparse and drooping. Needles are only retained on the tree for 2–4 years, so they are tufted near the ends of branches.

TWIGS. Gray to bluish-purple.

FRUIT: Large, woody cones; nearly round; 5–14" long; cone scales end in sharp, hooked claws. Weigh up to 2 pounds.

BARK: Thick on older trees; dark gray to black; furrowed with irregular plates and ridges.

Where it grows. Jeffrey pine has a limited range in the Northwest, growing only in the southwest corner of Oregon. However, it grows throughout California, sharing its range with ponderosa pine. Jeffrey pine can tolerate a wide variety of soils and widely fluctuating temperatures. It's one of the few trees that can grow on serpentine soils, whose high levels of calcium and magnesium are toxic to most plants.

Jeffrey pine cones and bushy needles

SIZE: Grows to 140′ tall and 4′ in diameter.

NEEDLES: Grow in bundles of three (rarely two); 5–10″ long; often "bushy" along twig.

FRUIT: Large, woody cones; 5–12″ long; each scale has a curved (J-shaped) prickle.

BARK: Flakes off in pieces like a jigsaw puzzle. Older bark is reddish-brown.

Uses. Jeffrey pine is used in the same ways as ponderosa pine and often is sold along with ponderosa pine as western yellow pine.

Three-needled pines

Use needles and cones together for the most accurate identification. Needle lengths and characteristics often overlap between these species. Some are primarily three-needled, but also have some bundles of two on the same tree. Cones, if present, are often the surest way to identify each species.

GRAY PINE
Needles are 6 to 13 inches long and distinctly gray-green. Cones are 6 to 10 inches long with thick, claw-like scales, especially near the base.

JEFFREY PINE
Needles are 5 to 11 inches long and blue-green with a white or purplish, waxy coating. Cones are 6 to 10 inches long and when open resemble a pineapple. Each scale has a sharp, curved prickle.

KNOBCONE PINE
Needles are 3 to 6 inches long and slender. Cones are 3 to 6 inches long and asymmetrical, with knoblike projections on the outer surface. They are typically whorled in groups of four to five around the branch or stem.

PONDEROSA PINE
Needles are 4 to 8 inches long, green, and sometimes in bundles of two. Cones are 3 to 6 inches long and egg-shaped when open. Each scale has a straight, pointed prickle.

Knobcone pine *Pinus attenuata*

A three-needled pine. Knobcone pine bears its 3- to 6-inch-long needles in groups of three. Individual needles can be straight or twisted. They are green and thinner than the other three-needled pines in the Northwest.

Knobcone pine cones grow singly or in whorls.

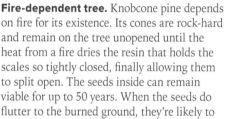

Prominent knobs of knobcone pine

Distinctive cones. It's hard to mistake the odd cones of knobcone pine. The side of each cone facing away from its woody branch is distinctly swollen and contains rock-hard, knoblike projections that give the tree its common name. Cones encircle the branches and trunk of the tree in dense, tightly clinging clusters, usually of four to five cones. These clusters can stay on the tree so long that they're overgrown by the wood — creating quite a surprise for woodcutters "bucking up" knobcone pine for firewood! And, these wood-enclosed clusters can still hold viable seeds.

Fire-dependent tree. Knobcone pine depends on fire for its existence. Its cones are rock-hard and remain on the tree unopened until the heat from a fire dries the resin that holds the scales so tightly closed, finally allowing them to split open. The seeds inside can remain viable for up to 50 years. When the seeds do flutter to the burned ground, they're likely to find the bright light and bare soil they need to flourish. Without fire, knobcone pines are eventually replaced by tree species that are more tolerant of shade. Knobcone has a short lifespan — often less than 60 to 100 years — and it does not age well, often falling apart as it ages.

Uses. Knobcone pine is a small, shrubby tree that commonly has many stems and many tops on each stem. Because of this, it's used primarily for firewood. It also helps pave the way for new forests following wildfire.

Range. Although knobcone pine grows throughout California, farther north it grows only in southwestern Oregon. Typically, it prefers hot, dry, low-elevation sites (1,000 to 2,000 feet) that are dominated by serpentine soils (high in magnesium) and frequented by wildfires.

SIZE: A small tree, typically 20–40' tall and under 2' in diameter. Often has multiple, crooked tops.

NEEDLES: Grow in bundles of three; 3–7" long; slender and straight or twisted.

FRUIT: Woody cones with swollen, knoblike bumps on one side; 3–6" long; grow in clusters of four to five.

BARK: Dark and scaly.

Knobcone pines often have multiple tops.

SIZE: Grows to 180' tall and 6' in diameter.

NEEDLES: Grow in bundles of three (rarely with two's intermixed); 5–10" long; tufted near the ends of branches.

FRUIT: Egg-shaped when open; 3–5" long; each scale has a straight, stiff prickle.

BARK: Flakes off in shapes like jigsaw puzzle pieces. Older trees have a distinct yellow or orange color.

Ponderosa pines, left; mature female cone, top; pollen cones ready to shed yellow pollen grains, bottom right; and juvenile female cones

Ponderosa pine *Pinus ponderosa*

The Northwest's No. 2 tree. Ponderosa pine is the most widely distributed pine in North America. It grows from the Pacific coast to South Dakota and from Canada to Mexico. It's Montana's state tree. In Oregon and Washington, it's almost as prominent east of the Cascades as Douglas-fir is west of that range. The scientific name of this tree, *Pinus ponderosa*, is almost the same as its common name. Lewis and Clark made note of this abundant pine in 1804, but it was David Douglas of Douglas-fir fame who named it in 1826. The name "ponderosa" refers to the ponderous or heavy wood. It has many common names in addition to ponderosa; many refer to particular growth characteristics at different ages and in different locations.

Recognizing ponderosa. Its needles are 4 to 10 inches long (depending on a combination of genetics and the sites on which it grows) and nearly always grow in bundles of three, but two's sometimes can be found mixed in with the three's. Groups of needles appear tufted at the ends of the branches, because the tree retains them for only 2 to 3 years before shedding them. Ponderosa's egg-shaped cones are 3 to 6 inches long, and each scale is tipped with a short, straight prickle. Cut branches and broken needles typically have a "pitchy" smell, similar to turpentine (this odor comes from chemicals called terpenes).

Unique bark. While the bark of young ponderosa pine is nearly black, the bark of mature trees is commonly pumpkin orange. In fact, large old trees are often called "punkins." As trees age, their bark flakes off in small, irregular pieces resembling the pieces of a jigsaw puzzle. At the base of old trees, look for piles of flaky bark; you'll discover the most fanciful shapes reminding you of all kinds of creatures.

Ponderosa pine is known for orange bark with a puzzle-like texture.

Where ponderosa pine grows. Ponderosa pine generally likes warm, sunny places, but it can tolerate severe winters. Productive forests grow with as little as 15 inches of annual rain. Almost half the trees east of the Cascade summit in Oregon and Washington are ponderosa pines. In southwest Oregon, ponderosa pine extends west into the Klamath-Siskiyou mountain complex. Surprising to many, ponderosa pines also are found scattered across Oregon's Willamette Valley, where they have a good ability to tolerate wet winter soils; these are typically referred to as "valley pines." In fact, many ponderosa plantations are being established on sites too wet for Douglas-fir. Ponderosa pine is long-lived, frequently exceeding 500 years; one in Oregon attained 726 years.

Uses. Ponderosa pine is prized for lumber and many other uses. In fact, the wood is claimed to be the most versatile of any found in North America. It's made into lumber for residential and other light construction, furniture, millwork (such as window frames, doors, stairs and molding), boxes and crates, and specialty items such as toys, fence pickets and slats. Its wood is often marketed as western yellow pine.

Unusual Oregon pines. Oregon's largest ponderosa pine (and one of the largest in the world) grows in LaPine State Park. A recent measurement placed it at 178 feet tall, with a diameter of nearly 9 feet; its age was estimated at 500 years. Northeastern Lake County has the "Lost Forest," a 9,000-acre island of ponderosa pine some 40 miles out in the desert. This strange grove exists on 10 inches of rain annually because special ground conditions trap moisture beneath the sandy soils.

Forests to enjoy. Ponderosa grows to a large size, and no other forest of our region can match the splendor of the older trees. Their bark fairly glows in the sunlight. There is enough color and beauty for a forest of make-believe where you might run into Hansel and Gretel or even Smokey Bear. Movie makers have long chosen the photogenic ponderosa forests for their forest scenes. Vacationers choose ponderosa country because this tree grows where the summer climate is most agreeable to people.

Fire in the forest. Ponderosa pine forests have evolved with fire. In fact, their health depends on it. Ponderosa forests grow in dry, grassy and shrubby environments where summer lightning and fires are common. If fires occur often enough, the stands stay thinned and healthy. If fires are inhibited by humans, stands become dense and stagnated. Individual trees become stressed and susceptible to insects (such as western pine beetles) and diseases (such as dwarf mistletoe). So when a fire finally does occur in a dense stand, many of the trees are killed.

When fires are not suppressed by humans, ponderosa pine forests experience small ground fires every 10 to 20 years. Most of the beautiful stands that people so admire in eastern Oregon owe their existence to frequent, light fires. Foresters often use low-intensity prescribed burns to manage ponderosa pine forests, both to enhance productivity and to lessen the damage from larger wildfires.

PHOTO: U.S. FOREST SERVICE

Ponderosa pine forests have evolved with fire. In fact, their health depends on it. Ponderosa forests grow in dry, grassy and brushy environments where summer lightning and the fires that result are common.

Telling ponderosa pine from Jeffrey pine

Among our three-needled pines, the two that are most often confused are ponderosa and Jeffrey. Here's how to tell them apart.

CONES. Cones are the best way to tell these two apart. Both are relatively large and egg-shaped. Jeffrey cones, however, are typically 5 to 12 inches long, and each cone scale ends in a prickle that curves in (said to be J-shaped). Ponderosa cones are typically 3 to 5 inches long, and their scales end in a straight prickle that sticks out. Roll the cones between your hands to feel the difference.

NEEDLES. Needles are similar for the two species, typically growing in bundles of three but sometimes two. In both species, they're typically 5 to 10 inches long. One difference is that ponderosa pine holds its needles for only two to three years, so they appear tufted near the ends of branches. Jeffrey pine holds its needles for five to eight years, so the branches often appear to be more bushy.

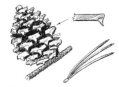

Ponderosa pine

Jeffrey pine

BARK. In both species, the bark flakes off in puzzle-like pieces. Some people detect a subtle difference in color in old trees: Jeffrey pine is reddish-brown, while ponderosa is yellow- or orange-brown. Some smell a difference: Jeffrey's bark smells sweet, like vanilla or pineapple, while ponderosa smells "pitchy," like turpentine.

TWIGS. Young twigs of Jeffrey pine are typically covered with a bluish-white or purplish-white bloom. Ponderosa twigs have no bloom: They are brown or green-brown.

Five-needled pines

- Use both needle and cone characteristics for the most accurate identification.
- Needles are often similar among the various species but may differ in length, stiffness, and the amount and type of stomatal bloom patterns.
- Cones, if present, are often the most distinctive characteristic.
- Where they grow in nature is an important aid in identification.
- All five-needled pines are subject to a deadly fungus called white pine blister rust.

MATT LAVIN

FOXTAIL PINE is a small tree of high elevations, growing almost exclusively in California. Needles are 1 to 1½ inches long, blue to yellow-green, and curve upward. Needles are retained on branches for many years (10 to 30 years), making the branches resemble a bushy fox's tail. Cones are egg-shaped and 2½ to 3½ inches long. The tips of cone scales are rounded and largely without prickles.

LIMBER PINE is a small to moderate sized tree of high elevations occurring sporadically in the Pacific Northwest but widespread throughout the West. Needles are 1½ to 3 inches long, dark yellow-green, and either straight or curved upward. Cones are 3 to 6 inches long and egg-shaped. Cone scales are thin and without prickles. Cones open when they are mature and fall from the tree.

SUGAR PINE is a large tree of mid-elevations, found mainly in California and southern Oregon. Needles are 2 to 4 inches long, blue-green, with multiple lines of stomatal bloom on all three surfaces; needle tips are pointed. Cones are 10 to 20 inches long, cylindrical and straight, with a long stalk. The ends of the cone scales are rounded and flat.

WESTERN WHITE PINE is a large tree of mid-elevations, widespread across the Pacific Northwest and the West. Needles are 1½ to 4 inches long, slender and flexible, and blue-green with multiple lines of white bloom on two of three surfaces. Cones are 4 to 10 inches long, cylindrical but curved like a banana. Cone scales curve up at the end and are often covered in white, sticky resin.

WHITEBARK PINE is a small tree of high elevations, widely distributed across mountains of the West and Pacific Northwest. Because of the harsh environment in which they grow, they are often twisted and stunted. Needles are 1 to 3 inches long, dark yellow-green, thick, often curved upward, and tufted near ends of branches. Cones are round to egg-shaped, 1½ to 3 inches long. Cone scales end with a distinct tooth and are typically covered with white, sticky resin. Cones remain closed on the tree until torn apart by birds or mammals seeking the high-energy seeds inside.

Foxtail pine *Pinus balfouriana*

Uncommon in Pacific Northwest forests. Primarily a tree of California, foxtail pines have a split population; one deeply embedded in the Coast Ranges of northern California and one in southern California in and around Sequoia and Kings Canyon National Parks. There are recent reports of it beginning to make

Foxtail pine with tightly bunched needles and few lateral branches

its way across the state line into southwestern Oregon; however, this is still controversial. Perhaps it will continue to march northward if the climate of the Northwest gets drier and warmer.

Why the name? Its short needles are retained on the branches for many years (10 to 30), and lateral branches are short or absent, giving some branches the appearance of a fox's tail.

Where it's found. In northern California this is a high-elevation species, typically found from 7,000 to 9,000 feet. Because there are few peaks this high in this area, foxtail pines often grow on isolated "sky islands." They most commonly grow on serpentine soils, although they do occur on other soil types. In the southern portion if its range, it occurs near tree line, 7,500 to 11,500 feet. Because of their small, scattered distributions, both populations are at risk from fires and climate change

A fire-prone environment. Although foxtail pines have not been studied extensively, they seem well-adapted to high-elevation fires — thick bark, thick trunk and branches, and often self-pruning branches. Their seeds are small with long wings, so wind helps them colonize sites that have been recently burned.

Long-lived. Though not as old as the more famous bristlecone pines, foxtail pines can live 1,500 to 3,400 years, making it one of the world's oldest trees species.

SIZE: Usually 20–50' tall. Trunks are usually single; seldom shrubby. Crowns are typically irregular, shaped by the harsh environment in which they grow. Branches short and thick.

NEEDLES: Clusters of five; ½–3½" long. Blue-green to yellow-green; typically curved upward. Many bushy branches that resemble a fox's tail.

FRUIT: Woody cones, 3–7" long; thick scales with few to no prickles. Seeds have terminal wings.

BARK: Thick; gray to orange-brown.

Limber pine *Pinus flexilis*

Uncommon in the Pacific Northwest. Limber pine is widespread throughout the Rocky Mountains and the high mountains of Nevada and Utah. It is uncommon in the Northwest although there is a small population in northeastern Oregon.

Small, five-needled pine. Limber pine is much smaller and much less common than sugar and western white pine, so those three are not likely to be confused. However, limber, foxtail, and whitebark

Limber pine branches can be tied in knots.

Limber pine

pines are quite similar — and all grow primarily at high elevations. So, they are easily confused. Limber pine gets its name from long, slender branches that are so flexible they can be tied in knots. Limber pine typically has a short, crooked trunk with many large, spreading branches.

Comparison with whitebark and foxtail pines. Limber and whitebark pines are easily confused. Where their ranges overlap in the northern Rockies, they grow in similar habitats, have similar growth forms, have five needles per fascicle, or bundle, and needles of similar length. Both begin life with a smooth, grayish-white bark, though limber pine bark darkens with age.

Cones are a principal difference. Limber pine cones generally are larger than whitebark cones and turn from green to brown as they ripen. When limber pine seeds are ripe, their cone scales open and the seeds fall to the ground. Once seeds are shed, the cones commonly fall to the ground still intact. Whitebark cones are usually smaller, remain purple throughout their development, and typically are picked to pieces by nutcrackers and jays while still on the tree. As a result, only pieces of whitebark cones are usually found on the ground. Both trees are important food sources for birds and small mammals and even for some larger ones, such as bears. Foxtail pine's needles tend to be shorter than the other two, and most needles curve upward from their branches.

Tree of high elevations. In the Northwest, limber pine grows only in the Wallowa Mountains of Oregon. It's typically found on open, windy ridges near tree line. Continually blasted by snow, ice, and sand, it often has a single upright stem surrounded by a low, dense, matted tangle of branches. Despite growing in harsh conditions, old trees may reach 1,000 to 2,000 years old.

SIZE: Usually 15–50' tall and up to 2' in diameter. Often shrubby at higher elevations.

NEEDLES: Clusters of five; 2–3" long; white lines on all surfaces.

FRUIT: Woody cones, 3–6" long; thick scales with no prickles. Light brown when mature. Seeds have short terminal wings.

BARK: Grayish-brown with furrows and ridges.

Sugar pine *Pinus lambertiana*

Look for big cones. Both western white pine and sugar pine are tall, stately trees that bear their needles in bundles of five (other five-needled pines in the Northwest are much shorter and often stunted). Sugar pine's huge cones make it easy to identify. They typically measure 10 to 18 inches long and dangle from the tips of long upper limbs, bending them downward like a stubborn fish pulling on a fishing pole. Green cones can weigh 3 or 4 pounds, and it's "bombs away!" when squirrels drop them from 100 feet up — campers beware! Though sugar pine is common throughout mid-elevation forests of southwest Oregon and most of California, it seldom grows in pure stands. It prefers moist, well-drained spots in the sun and grows mixed with other conifers, especially Douglas-fir and ponderosa pine.

Large sugar pine

"The priests of pine." John Muir, the famous early-American naturalist, greatly admired sugar pine. Observing these large trees in the forest, he wrote, "They are ever tossing out their immense arms in what might seem the most extravagant gestures. ... They are the priests of pine and seem ever to be addressing the surrounding forest. ... The yellow pine is found growing with them on warm hillsides, and the white silver fir on cool northern slopes; but noble as these are, the sugar pine is easily king and spreads his arm above them in blessing while they nod and wave in signs of recognition."

A long, straight sugar pine cone

What it's used for. Sugar pine belongs to a group of pines known as soft or white pines, named for their light, soft, easily worked, high-value wood. Currently, its wood is used primarily for millwork that surrounds doors and windows. Its wood is similar to that of western white pine, so they are commonly marketed together.

A narrow escape. David Douglas, the young Scottish botanist for whom Douglas-fir is named, found himself in great danger on the day he found his first sugar pine in the field (October 26, 1826). Near Oregon City he had seen large pine seeds in a Northwest Indian's pouch, and he had gone into southern Oregon in search of the tree that grew such huge seeds. Near what is now Roseburg, Douglas found the tree. To get some of the cones, which he said hung from their branches "like small sugar loaves in a grocer's shop," he shot them down with his gun. Attracted by the noise, several local Indians came to investigate the commotion. Although there are several accounts of this meeting, it seems that Douglas felt threated and drew his rifle and pistol to ensure his safety. It worked to head off any conflict, and Douglas retreated at his first opportunity.

SIZE: Commonly reaches 100–200′ tall, but may exceed 250′; diameters reach to 7′. The tallest of all the pines in the world.

NEEDLES: Five needles per cluster; 2–4″ long; stomatal bloom (white lines) on all three surfaces of each needle.

FRUIT: Huge, woody cones (10–20″ long) with thin scales and long stalks. Tips of the scales often drip with sticky resin.

BARK: Reddish-brown and furrowed (no blocky patches, and no rings where whorls of branches once grew).

BLISTER RUST: Like all five-needled pines, sugar pine is susceptible to white pine blister rust.

Furrowed bark of sugar pine

Taste treat. The cones of sugar pine are the longest of any pine in the world, although they're not as heavy as the fearsome, spiny cones of California's Coulter pine. Their seeds are also large, and very tasty. Each seed is as big as a kernel of corn and has a terminal wing from 1 to 2 inches long. The name "sugar pine" comes from the sugary-tasting globules of resin that drip from wounds to the trunk or branches. Northwest Indians were fond of this resin, but they were careful not to eat too much of it because of its laxative effect. Sugar pines sometimes grow more than 200 feet tall and 10 feet in diameter — making it the tallest and most massive of all the world's pines.

Western white pine

Pinus monticola

Five-needled pine. Like sugar pine, western white pine is a tall, stately tree of mid-elevations, with needles borne in fascicles (bundles) of five. The other five-needled pines of Northwest forests are much shorter in stature and typically occur near tree line.

Distinctive cones. The cones of western white pine are one of its most distinctive features. They range in length from 5 to 12 inches, and they commonly have a graceful curve, similar to a banana. Their scales are thin, turned up on the end, and are commonly covered with white, sticky resin.

Uses. Carpenters enjoy working with western white pine because it has a light, smooth, attractive wood that planes and saws easily. It's similar to eastern white pine, the top-ranked American wood for nearly 300 years. Western white pine has many important uses, much like those listed for ponderosa pine. Interestingly, most wooden matches are made of western white pine, and it's a favorite of woodcarvers.

Western white pine

SIZE: Mature trees commonly reach 100–165' tall and sometimes exceed 200'; diameters reach 4'.

NEEDLES: Grow in clusters of five; 2–4" long; white lines of stomatal bloom occur on 2 sides of each needle.

FRUIT: Woody cones, 5–12" long; slender and curved like a banana. Cone scales are thin and often curve up on the end; they stay thin and flexible (especially when compared with sugar pine.

BARK: Dark; broken into squares or rectangles on older trees. Bark often appears "ringed" where a whorl of branches once grew, even long after the branches have fallen from the tree.

More about white pine. Although it grows at middle elevations throughout much of the Northwest, western white pine does not usually grow in pure stands. Instead, it grows in mixed forests along with Douglas-fir, true firs and several other pines. To determine its age, simply count the whorls of limbs on a white pine, and you will know how old it is (one whorl per year of growth — but you also need to add in the number of whorls that have died and fallen from the tree over time). Douglas-fir and most true firs show this habit too, but often less clearly. Western white pine is the state tree of Idaho, and its scientific name, *monticola,* means "of the mountains."

Tree-killing fungus. White pine blister rust is a fungus that attacks and kills all five-needled pines; it was accidentally introduced into North America from Europe in 1909. Because it must spend one stage of its life on leaves of currant and gooseberry bushes, a great effort was made in the mid-1900s to eliminate these shrubs from the forest. However, this proved unworkable; wind-blown rust spores travel too far and too fast.

Some estimates suggest that 90% of white pines west of the Cascade crest have been killed by this fungus. However, rust-resistant strains do occur in nature, and foresters and scientists are working with this genetic resistance to improve white pine's chances of survival — with significant success.

Rectangular pattern of western white pine bark

How to tell western white pine from sugar pine

Our five-needled pines are difficult to tell apart without looking at a lot of clues. But the two that cause the most problems are the large, commercially important species: sugar pine and western white pine. Here's how to tell them apart.

■ **CONES.** These are the best way to tell these two species apart. Western white pine cones are typically 5 to 12 inches long, slender and curved, like a banana. Their scales are thin and turn up on the ends. Sugar pine cones are much larger — typically 10 to 20 inches long. They're also much fatter and straighter than western white pine cones. Their scales are typically thick and straight.

■ **BARK.** The bark of large western white pines is broken into small squares that resemble bathroom tile or the back of an alligator. Its color is dark gray to black. Also, there are commonly rings around the trunk left over from where whorls of branches once circled the tree. On large sugar pine trees, its reddish-brown bark is broken into long ridges and furrows. The whorls of former branches around the trunk are much less obvious. The bark of sugar pine begins to break up into narrow plates on trees as small as 4 inches in diameter, while the bark of white pine remains smooth on young trees.

■ **NEEDLES.** In both species, each single needle has three sides. (When the 5 needles in each fascicle are carefully put back together, they form a single round needle.) In sugar pine, each side of each needle has several white lines of stomatal bloom. In western white pine, only two sides have white lines, but they are often brighter than on sugar pine.

Western white pine

PHOTO: S. RAE

Sugar pine

Whitebark pine *Pinus albicaulis*

Small, five-needled pine. Whitebark pine is similar in appearance to limber pine, but its cones are smaller than those of limber pine, and it's much more widely distributed in Oregon and Washington than is limber pine. When mature, the cones of whitebark pine are purple, and they stay on the tree with scales closed for at least 1 year. The seeds are unwinged and resemble small pebbles, which is why whitebark is classified as a stone pine. The bark of whitebark pine stays grayish-white throughout its life, giving rise to its common name. Like limber pine, its twigs are as flexible as rope.

Birds and bears. The life cycle of whitebark pine is integrally linked to that of Clark's nutcrackers (and several other species of jays). These long-beaked birds are able to reach inside the scales of mature whitebark pine cones and pluck out the ripe seeds, while most other animals need to tear apart the cones to get at the seeds. Many of the seeds are eaten immediately and form a vital food source for these birds, but many more are stored in the

Whitebark pine

SIZE: Usually under 50' tall and 2' in diameter. Often distorted or shrub-like.

NEEDLES: Clusters of five; 1–3" long; dark yellow-green with faint white lines on all surfaces. Often curved upward.

FRUIT: Woody, egg-shaped cones; 2½ to 3½" long; most cone scales end in a distinct tooth. Cones remain on the tree, closed, for many years.

BARK: Thin, scaly and light gray.

ground for later use (perhaps as many as 10,000 seeds per acre!). Some sprout there, forming the basis for a new population of pine trees. As a result, Clark's nutcrackers and whitebark pines are almost totally dependent on each other for survival. Birds with shorter, thicker beaks, and sharp-toothed mammals, must break the scales off to get at the seeds held tightly inside. The seeds of this pine are also critical for the survival of grizzly bears, who gorge on the fatty seeds to lay-on fat prior to winter hibernation. As the survival of whitebark pine is threatened by white pine blister rust, so too are the grizzly bears who depend on them.

Found in the Cascades. Whitebark pine grows near tree line throughout the Cascades and in the northern Rockies, clinging to the harshest sites that trees can endure. While it can tolerate terrific cold and wind, it's usually distorted and bushlike. Timberline trees no taller than an adult person have been found to be 500 to 1,000 years old.

Although redwoods once occurred globally, they are now limited to the coastlines of northern California and southwestern Oregon.

Redwoods *Sequoia*

Redwoods have an interesting taxonomic history. Although several species of redwood (*Sequoia*) once spread across the globe, long-term changes in climate and environment have dramatically reduced their numbers and their range. Now, only one species exists, *Sequoia sempervirens*, and it occupies a narrow band along the West Coast of North America, from southwestern Oregon to Big Sur, California.

Two other trees are commonly confused with redwoods, but each is a separate genus: giant sequoia, *Sequoiadendron* (often called Sierra redwood), and dawn redwood, *Metasequoia*. Before the Cascades formed, when Oregon's climate was warmer and wetter, all three "redwoods" grew here. Now, giant sequoia is native only to California, while dawn redwood is native only to China. However, each of these trees is widely planted in temperate regions around the world; each is described briefly in "Common Ornamental Trees," page 117.

Redwood *Sequoia sempervirens*

Often called coast redwood to distinguish it
from Sierra redwood, *Sequoiadendron giganteum*

Limited range. Although redwoods are commonly associated with
low- to mid-elevation forests along the coast of northern and central
California, they also cross the border into southwest Oregon —
although there, they are confined to a few mountain slopes and river
valleys in Curry County. Before the Cascades formed, redwoods grew
throughout the Pacific Northwest.

What's in a name? The common name, redwood, comes from the
reddish-brown color of the heartwood — very resistant to damage
from insects and decay. The Latin name for the genus, *Sequoia,* honors
Chief Sequoyah, the Cherokee Indian who invented an alphabet for
his people. The species name, *sempervirens,* means evergreen, perhaps
in reference to its foliage or perhaps because of its tendency to sprout
vigorously following injury from fire, cutting, or other types of
mechanical damage. At one time, this genus included giant sequoia,
but after much botanical debate, giant sequoia was placed in its own
genus, *Sequoiadendron.* Now "cousins," the two species commonly are
grouped together under the name California redwood and together are
the state tree of California.

How to know redwood. On most twigs, the leaves are needle-like,
about 1 inch long, and lie in two flat rows. Each is shaped like a
double-edged sword. Needles become uniformly shorter near both
ends of the twig. On branches that bear cones, needles may be shaped
like sewing awls — short, sharp and rapidly tapering. Redwood cones
are cylindrical, generally under 1 inch long, and are made up of thick,
wrinkled scales. Bark is distinctive: reddish brown, thick, fibrous, and
deeply furrowed.

Uses. The wood is said to have "just about every characteristic that
makes for the ideal." It has color, beauty, great resistance to insects
and decay, and other special qualities. Further, large sizes and
clear material are readily available. House siding, interior paneling,
laminated structural timbers, and shingles and shakes are leading
uses. Among the many specialty products are wine vats, greenhouse

SIZE: Grows to
370′ tall and 23′ in
diameter.

NEEDLES: About
1″ long; both tops
and bottoms have
several bands of
white stomatal bloom,
although tops often
appear green; grow
in a flat plane; end in
a distinct, but soft,
point. Needles vary in
size, with the longest
in the middle of each
twig, tapering to each
end.

FRUIT: Small, woody
cones about 1″ long;
thick, wrinkled scales.

TWIGS: Green at first,
but turn brown after
several years. No leaf
scars present. Twigs
and leaves are shed
intact (as a single
unit).

BARK: Very thick (up
to 12″); reddish-brown
and fibrous.

**Redwood bark and two-ranked needles. Although red and fibrous
when young, redwood bark darkens and thickens with age, becoming
good protection against fire.**

frames, fences, and outdoor furniture. Bark products include insulation, mulch, and chemicals. Because of these features, redwoods not preserved in parks and other natural areas are still actively logged and replanted.

Redwood cone

Famous tree. Despite its limited range (less than 0.2% of U.S. commercial forest land), redwood is a world-famous tree. Its magnificent size, the density of its stands, and the astonishing longevity of individuals trees (many surpass 1,000 years old), combine to place redwoods at the center of a worldwide conservation movement. As a result, approximately 80% of the redwood forests are protected in national, state and local parks. While protected from logging, they are, of course, still at risk from wildfire, insects, diseases and storms.

Natural enemies. Redwood has few natural enemies. Chemicals stored in its heartwood protect it from most insects and diseases. Soft, spongy bark that commonly reaches 12 inches thick protects it from all but the most severe fires. The ability to sprout both roots and shoots from its trunk helps it recover from mud deposits that commonly occur in its flood-prone, river-bottom habitat. The ability to sprout also helps it regenerate following logging and fires.

Spruces *Picea*

Many people think that spruces, Douglas-firs and true firs look alike. In a general way they do, but look more closely. Feel the needles. Spruces have stiff, prickly needles; Douglas-firs and true firs have soft, flexible needles. If you dropped from an airplane into a Northwest forest and felt tree needles sticking you like pins, the tree would likely be a spruce. Each spruce needle springs from a tiny, woody peg; in fact, this peg is one of the best ways to identify a spruce. Spruce cones hang down from the branches like Douglas-fir cones (true fir cones stand upright), but spruce cones do not have Douglas-fir's pitchfork bracts. The scales of most spruce cones are papery thin. The bark of mature spruces is scaly and flaky, while the bark of mature Douglas-fir and the true firs is typically ridged and not flaky.

There are approximately 40 different species of spruce in the world, but only three are native to the Pacific Northwest, and only two of those are common. Location is probably the best clue to their identity, because their

Engelmann spruce in the high Cascades

ranges seldom overlap, but needles, cones and growth form also provide helpful clues.

- **Brewer spruce** grows only in the Siskiyou Mountains of southwestern Oregon and northern California. Needles typically are square in cross-section and are blunt on their ends. Branches typically dangle and weep.

Brewer spruce needles

- **Engelmann spruce** grows only in the Cascades and Rocky Mountains, from central British Columbia through New Mexico, and only at mid- to high elevations. Needles typically are square in cross-section and range from being very sharp to blunt.

- **Sitka spruce** typically grows within 10 to 50 miles of the Pacific coast, from southeastern Alaska to northern California. It grows only near sea level. Needles are often (but not always) flattened in cross-section and are typically very sharp. Sitka spruce is among the world's fastest growing trees.

Engelmann spruce needles

A note about white spruce: White spruce spans Canada and the northeastern portion of the United States. In the western United States, it dips into the northern Rockies of Montana. There are reports of white spruce also occurring in Washington, but sources differ on this. White spruce is described in "Common Ornamental Trees," page 117.

Sitka spruce needles

Brewer spruce *Picea breweriana*

Also called Brewer's weeping spruce

Unique to southwestern Oregon and northern California. Brewer spruce is a little-known tree that grows only on steep mountain slopes in the Siskiyou Mountains of southern Oregon and northern California.

Why does it weep? Does this strange tree mourn because so few people ever push into the high solitude of Josephine and Curry counties to glimpse its beauty? Stringlike branchlets 4 to 8 feet long hang down from its limbs. It's a scarce tree, but you probably would recognize it and be reminded of a weeping willow, or a very shaggy dog.

To tell it from other spruces. Its needles resemble those of Engelmann spruce, only they're even more blunt to the touch. Its cones are 3 to 6 inches long — longer than either of the Northwest's two other spruces — and its cone scales are smooth rather than jagged. Its long, weeping branches are perhaps its most distinctive characteristic.

Brewer spruce

SIZE: May reach 80–100′ tall and 2–4′ in diameter.

NEEDLES: 1″ long; triangular; blunt tips; dark green with lines of stomatal bloom above but not below; point toward twig tip.

FRUIT: Woody cones; 3–5″ long; stiff, rounded scales with smooth edges.

TWIGS: Branches are long and drooping. Twigs covered with distinct, woody pegs.

BARK: Thin; reddish-brown; scaly.

Susceptible to fire. Although it grows in a fire-prone environment, Brewer spruce has thin bark, shallow roots, and drooping branches, so it is easily damaged even by low-intensity fires. As a result, it is often found growing on open, rocky ridges where it's hard to carry a fire. It is quite tolerant of shade, so is found in late-successional stands.

Engelmann spruce *Picea engelmannii*

Similar to Sitka spruce. The cones and needles of Engelmann spruce are similar to those of Sitka spruce. Even so, Engelmann needles are usually (but not always) less sharp, point uniformly toward the tip of the twig, and are definitely four-sided (Sitka needles are flatter). Because they're nearly square, Engelmann needles roll easily between your fingers — and because they're flatter, Sitka's needles don't. Also, Engelmann needles have an unpleasant odor when crushed. Cones of the two species are similar.

Engelmann spruce cones and flaky bark

Size and use.
Engelmann spruce is a much smaller tree than its coastal cousin. Most fall short of 100 feet in height and 3 feet in diameter. The wood is used for lumber, and like other spruces, it has superior paper-making properties. It's also used to make the finest violins in the world.

Range. Range is the best way to distinguish Engelmann from Sitka spruce. Engelmann ordinarily grows above 4,000 feet, often in cold, wet environments. Therefore, it's not found in the Coast Range of Oregon and Washington. Farther inland, it grows from Canada to Mexico.

Shade-tolerant tree. That means it will grow in its own shade or the shade of other trees. That's why you'll find Engelmann spruce — little trees and big ones — closely mixed. Branches are held on the trunk nearly to the ground except in very dense stands.

SIZE: Grows to 150′ tall and 3′ in diameter.

NEEDLES: 1″ long; sharp; blue-green; tend to point forward; are usually square in cross section and roll easily between the fingers; unpleasant odor when crushed.

FRUIT: Woody cones 1–3″ long; very thin scales with jagged edges; hang down.

TWIGS: Covered with distinct, raised pegs.

BARK: Thin; gray with purple tinge; scaly.

The underside of Engelmann spruce needles

Sitka spruce *Picea sitchensis*

Knowing Sitka spruce. Fortunately, the Northwest's two most common and similar spruces, Sitka and Engelmann, grow in separate parts of the region, because they're often difficult to tell apart. Sitka spruce grows naturally only along the coast, and Engelmann spruce grows only in the mountains — although both are planted in other regions. If the two trees did grow together, you would have to look carefully to tell them apart. Sitka needles are truly "needles" — the stiffest and sharpest of any tree in our region. In addition, Sitka needles are flat, so they don't roll easily between your finger and thumb; and needles on top of the twig point forward, but those at the side point outward. Engelmann needles are not usually as sharp, are four-sided (will roll easily) and all point slightly forward.

Sitka spruce

Where Sitka grows. Sitka spruce likes the cool, foggy environment of the Pacific Northwest's coast. In fact, it is sometimes called tideland spruce. In Oregon, it's seldom found more than a few miles inland. In Washington, Alaska and British Columbia, it ranges farther inland, but still hugs the coast. Sitka spruce is the largest species of spruce in the world — with diameters of the largest trees commonly exceeding 15 feet! Its seedlings often find a home on downed logs and stumps (called nurse logs). In several hundred years, when the nurse log rots away, the Sitka spruces often appear to be growing on stilts. Sitka spruce was named after Sitka Island (now called Baranof Island) off the coast of Alaska. It is Alaska's state tree.

A wood with special qualities. Sitka spruce wood is very strong for its weight, which leads to many specialty uses such as ladders, aircraft shells, racing shells, garage doors, and folding bleachers. Sitka spruce is also used in pianos, organs and violins because of its outstanding resonant qualities. Its lumber is also valued for a wide range of familiar purposes. Of the paper-making woods, western hemlock and Sitka spruce are kings. Their long fibers make a strong newsprint of good color and printing qualities.

Cone-like galls. Sitka spruces (as well as other spruces) are commonly infected by an insect know as Cooley spruce gall aphid. The resulting galls resemble cones with needles sticking out from them. Although they can be unsightly, they don't seem to harm the tree (other than the growth of the branches they infect).

Unique silhouette. When driving to the coast, it's interesting to pick out the first spruce to appear. Individuals growing in the open are unmistakable — limbs thrust out rigidly like long, pointing arms, each trailing a triangular fringe of branchlets.

SIZE: Commonly grows to 180' tall and 5' in diameter, although individuals may reach almost 300' tall and 16' in diameter.

NEEDLES: 1" long; sharp; yellow-green to blue-green with two broad white bands of stomatal bloom below; often flat (difficult to roll between your fingers). Some needles on a twig point sideways, others point forward.

FRUIT: Woody cones; 2–4" long; hang down; very thin scales with jagged edges.

TWIGS: Each needle is borne on a raised, woody peg (called a sterigma).

BARK: Thin; gray-brown; scaly.

Sitka spruce cone and needles, at top, and aphid gall

True firs *Abies*

True firs are so named to distinguish them from Douglas-firs, Chinese-firs, and a number of other pretenders. Sometimes they're called "balsam firs" because of tiny pockets of resin, or balsam, that lie within their bark. About 40 species of true firs grow in cold regions of the northern hemisphere. True firs are well adapted to snowy environments because their short, stiff branches and pointed tops shed snow without breaking.

Seven species of true fir are native to western North America, and the Northwest has six — more than any other region of North America. Here are the Northwestern true firs:

- California red fir (and a variety of it, Shasta red fir)
- Grand fir
- Noble fir
- Pacific silver fir
- Subalpine fir
- White fir

Many consider true firs to be the loveliest of conifers. Scottish botanist David Douglas first used the admiring names borne by so many of our true firs: noble, grand, *amabilis* (lovely), and *magnifica* (magnificent).

Subalpine fir in Olympic National Park, Washington

California red fir *Abies magnifica*

California red fir

Looks like noble fir. California red fir and noble fir are nearly identical. Both are called red firs because of their reddish-brown twigs. Both have needles that are shaped like hockey sticks, with bloom on their upper and lower surfaces, and tend to cluster on the upper sides of the twigs. One difference is that California red fir needles have a tiny ridge rising along the length of their upper surface, while noble firs have a tiny groove. Cones are the best way to tell them apart; although similar in size and shape, California red fir cones do not have "whiskers" as noble fir cones do.

Primarily in California. California red fir is essentially a California species. In Oregon

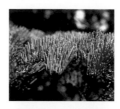

it grows only in the southern third of the Cascades and at the highest elevations in the Siskiyous. It typically grows above 4,500 feet, thriving in areas of heavy snow and long winters. North of Crater Lake, most red firs are noble firs; south of Mount Shasta, most are California red firs. In between they may be either — or a combination — because they hybridize where their ranges overlap; this hybrid is called Shasta red fir, and it shares characteristics from both parents. Neither California red fir nor Shasta red fir grow north of central Oregon.

Majestic tree. Splendid groves of large, old California red firs enhance Sierra playgrounds like Yosemite. The rich red-brown bark of these oldsters draws an appreciative eye. John Muir considered this tree "the most charmingly symmetrical of all the giants of the Sierra woods." The species name, *magnifica,* captures the grandeur of this tree. California red fir and its close relative, Shasta red fir, are prized as Christmas trees because of their symmetrical shape and bluish foliage.

Shasta red fir. Hybrids between noble fir and California red fir are commonly called Shasta red fir because they're so common near Mount Shasta in northern California. These trees typically have intermediate characteristics: cones that are only partially "shingled" by protruding papery bracts, and needles that are both grooved and ridged. The scientific name of the hybrid is *Abies magnifica* var. *shastensis.*

California red fir needles, cone and needle scars on twig

SIZE: Grows to 200' tall and 5' in diameter.

NEEDLES: White on both surfaces; shaped like a hockey stick. Massed on the upper surface of the twig. A tiny ridge runs the length of the upper side.

FRUIT: Large, woody cone (6–9" long); cylindrical; bracts are shorter than scales (therefore not visible). Fall apart at maturity as seeds ripen.

TWIGS: Reddish brown. Buds clustered at the terminal end are generally not covered with resin.

BARK: Blistered on young trees. Reddish brown and deeply furrowed on mature trees.

Grand fir *Abies grandis*

Widespread fir. Grand fir is the Northwest's only true fir commonly found below 1,500 feet. Knowing this helps to identify it in western Oregon and Washington, where it is sometimes called lowland white fir. However, it's a mountaineer too, ranging up to 5,000 feet in the mountains of eastern Oregon and Washington. A rover, grand fir is found throughout most of Oregon and Washington. Its habit is to mingle with other conifers and not to form pure stands, so its numbers are modest — perhaps 2% of our coniferous trees. Grand fir prefers moist locations and so is common near streams, in valleys, and on lower slopes. East of the Cascades, it's common in the mixed forest types found at middle elevations. Grand fir is very tolerant of shade, so it can form climax forests throughout much of its range.

Grand fir cones

Recognizing true firs

ALL TRUE FIRS have the following characteristics:

- Cones that perch like little owls on the topmost branches. Look aloft for large, erect cones. They often glisten with drops of fragrant, sticky resin.

- Cones of true firs do not fall intact from the tree like most other conifer cones. In late fall, their scales tumble off one by one when the seeds have ripened. As a result, cones can be used to recognize true firs only in summer and early fall.

- Twig scars. Gently pull a needle away from its twig and notice the tiny, flat, circular scar left on the twig. This circle makes it easy to recognize a true fir at any season.

- Young stems contain fragrant resin blisters. Poke them with your finger and they'll pop, oozing a clear, sticky liquid. Resins and oils from the bark and foliage of true firs are used for a variety of products, including perfumes, adhesives and pharmaceuticals. Some attribute a healing effect to this liquid. While inside the tree, resin helps protect the tree from insects and diseases.

- The buds of true firs are typically rounded and are often covered with resin, wax or curved needles. Buds near the ends of twigs often grow in clusters of three or more.

Commercial uses

True firs account for about 10% of the commercial timber in Oregon and Washington. They're used for lumber and plywood, and their wood fibers make superior paper. In North America, their lumber is often mixed with hemlock and sold as "Hem-Fir," but it's shipped to eastern Asia by itself where it's prized for its light color. Many older, larger true firs are infected with fungi that cause rot in the tree; this often limits their use for dimensional lumber. True firs are among our most popular Christmas trees because of their soft, fragrant foliage and their symmetrical shapes.

Telling true firs apart

Distinguishing between the different species of true firs is one of the most challenging tree identification tasks in Northwest forests. It takes patience and practice. To make things even harder, several of our species interbreed, resulting in offspring that have characteristics of both parents. Needle shape and color, twig color, the size, shape, and color of cones, and where the trees grow in the forest are all helpful in identifying the true firs. Start by looking to see where bloom (white or bluish-white color) occurs on the needles, then look for the other characteristics listed below.

If the needles have bloom on only the lower surface, then it's either grand fir or Pacific silver fir.

The cones of true firs don't fall intact from the tree. Scales fall away after seeds ripen.

- If all the needles point to the side and grow in two distinct rows (either flat or V-shaped), then it's grand fir. Grand fir typically grows at lower elevations than Pacific silver fir. If you can find a cone on the tree, it's slender and brown at maturity.

- If the needles do not grow in two distinct rows (if the topmost needles point forward) then it's Pacific silver fir. Pacific silver fir typically grows at higher elevations than grand fir. If you can find a cone on the tree, it's quite stout and purple, regardless of age.

If the needles have bloom on both sides (top and bottom), then it's either noble fir, California red fir, subalpine fir, or white fir. Read the following statements to decide which it's most likely to be.

- If the needles are shaped like hockey sticks and the young twigs are reddish brown, it's either noble fir or California red fir.

  - **If the cones are wrapped in whiskery spirals,** then it's noble fir. If you don't have cones to look at, look at a single needle. If you see a groove on top of the needle, it's likely to be a noble fir. Although their ranges overlap near the Oregon-California border, noble fir becomes more common the farther north you are from that border; and only noble fir grows in Washington.

  - **If the cones are not wrapped in whiskery spirals,** then it's California red fir. Again, if you don't have a cone, look at a single needle. If it's flat or ridged on top, it's likely to be a California red fir. Although their ranges overlap, California red fir is more common the farther south you are from the Oregon-California border.

- If the needles are mostly straight and the young twigs are greenish, then it's either white fir or subalpine fir.

  - **If most needles are less than 1 inch long** and are tightly spaced on the twig, then it's subalpine fir. Subalpine fir grows at high elevations, all the way to tree line. Mature cones are most often purple.

  - **If most needles are over 1½ inches long** and are loosely spaced on the twig, then it's white fir. White fir tends to grow at mid-elevations. Mature cones are brown.

Recognizing grand fir. Try to identify grand fir by the foliage of its lower branches. Here, the needles will be shiny green on top (no white bloom) and will be arranged in two flattened rows, as if pressed in a book. When growing in bright light, the rows of needles may turn up and form a V, but they still appear to be parted down

A stand of grand fir, top; bark, bottom right; and needles

the middle. The needles of grand fir are especially easy to confuse with Douglas-fir, but the buds and cones make it easy to tell them apart. Grand fir buds are round, and its cones grow upright; Douglas-fir buds are pointed, and its cones hang down. In eastern and southwestern Oregon, it's often difficult to tell grand fir from white fir, for they interbreed and their offspring have characteristics of both species.

Uses. Grand fir's maximum life span of 250 to 300 years is rather short for a western conifer. Yet it grows rapidly in its youth and may attain reasonably large sizes. On some Cascade and Blue Mountain sites, its fast growth rate makes it a preferred timber species. Grand fir wood is used in the same way as the other true firs. It's also an important Christmas tree because of its lovely form, its appealing fragrance and its rich green color.

Disease problems. Unlike Douglas-fir and most pines, the wood of true firs is not resinous — it does not exude pitch to seal off wounds — so decay-causing fungi find easy entrance. Grand fir, particularly, is subject to trunk rots. The "Indian paint" fungus often seen on grand fir east of the Cascades catches the eye. Its black conks (growths on the trunk) have brick-red insides and were used by Northwest Indians for pigments.

Noble fir *Abies procera*

Recognizing noble fir. If there are cones on the tree, noble fir is the easiest true fir to identify in Northwest forests. As with all true firs, noble fir cones sit upright on their branches, are barrel-shaped, have thin scales with rounded "shoulders," and fall apart in the late fall after the seeds have ripened. One feature sets noble fir cones apart from the others: they're wrapped in "whiskery spirals." These whiskers are actually paper-thin bracts that separate the seeds from the cone scales. All conifers have them, but noble fir is one of the

SIZE: Grows to 250′ tall and 6′ in diameter (but typically smaller).

NEEDLES: No bloom on upper surface; two bands on the underside. Sets of needles flattened (in shade) or V-shaped (in sun).

FRUIT: Upright, cylindrical cones; 3–5″ long; bracts shorter than scales. Green when young; brown when mature. Fall apart when mature, leaving a pencil-like spike on the branch.

TWIGS: Terminal buds are clustered in three's or more and are covered with resin. Young twigs are greenish.

BARK: 2–3″ thick; gray-brown and moderately furrowed; inner bark is reddish-brown.

Noble fir bark

few species where they're long enough to extend outside the cone (Douglas-fir is another example).

Needles and twigs. Needles and twigs also help identify noble fir. Needles are white on both upper and lower surfaces and curve at the base like a hockey stick. Unlike other true firs (except California red fir in southern Oregon and northern California), each needle runs parallel to the twig for about 1/8 inch before it curves away. To

Whiskery cones and a stand of large noble fir at Marys Peak, Oregon

distinguish noble fir from California red fir, look for cones, if you can find them; if not, look for a tiny groove that runs the length of the upper surface of the needle — that's noble fir. Young noble fir twigs are a distinct reddish brown, and the up-curved, densely massed needles are different from other true firs. When growing in the sun, needles are tightly packed on the upper half of the twig, almost as if they'd been neatly combed. When growing in the shade, the needles may flatten out, or take on the look of a Mohawk haircut. The foliage of noble fir is so handsome that one heavy branch with a red ribbon attached makes a perfect Christmas door swag.

Where it grows. Noble fir is truly a tree of the Pacific Northwest. It's common at middle and upper elevations in the western Cascades of Washington and the northern three-fourths of Oregon. It is much less common in the Coast Ranges of Oregon and Washington, and only from Marys Peak, Oregon, northward.

Uses. A fine timber species, noble fir has very strong wood for its weight. It's also one of our most popular Christmas trees and gets some use as an ornamental because of its blue color, its symmetrical growth pattern, and its unique cones. Along the Columbia Gorge there is a mountain covered in noble firs. But because the wood of most firs is not highly valued, it's called "Larch Mountain." Local wisdom suggests that it was named Larch Mountain back in the day so the wood could be sold as larch rather than fir.

An apt name. David Douglas "discovered" and named noble fir in 1825, paying tribute to its magnificent and noble form.

SIZE: Grows to 230' tall and 5' in diameter.

NEEDLES: White on both surfaces; shaped like a hockey stick. Massed on the upper surface of the twig. A tiny groove runs the length of the upper side.

FRUIT: Large, woody cone (4–8" long); cylindrical; has distinctive bracts that look a bit like elephant heads. Cone falls apart at maturity to help the seeds fall.

TWIGS: Reddish-brown. Buds clustered at the terminal end are overlapped by curved needles.

BARK: Blistered on young trees. Purplish-gray to reddish-brown on mature trees; flattened ridges.

Pacific silver fir *Abies amabilis*

Useful name. Although the upper surface of each needle is entirely green, the underside is silvery white, giving rise to the common name, silver fir. Often, they seem to gleam as brightly as bicycle reflectors. The bark of trees less than 3 feet in diameter is also silvery, but as the tree ages, the bark turns dark gray-brown and develops ridges and furrows. In some places, foresters consider the bark alone a reliable means of identification.

A stand of Pacific silver fir, top; characteristic large, blue cones, bottom right; and needles, which are green on top and silvery below.

SIZE: Commonly grow to 100–230' tall and up to 4' in diameter.

NEEDLES: Green on top and shiny white underneath. Top needles point forward like ski jumpers.

FRUIT: Large woody cones (3–6" long); purple. Fall apart at maturity.

TWIGS: Greenish. Buds are clustered at tips of twigs; purple; and covered with pitch.

BARK: Remains gray throughout its life; smooth with resin blisters when young but ridged and furrowed and without blisters when older.

Recognizing silver fir. Unlike most true firs (except grand), Pacific silver fir's needles are green on top (no white bloom). To distinguish Pacific silver fir from grand fir, look at the needles on top of each twig. In Pacific silver fir, they lean forward like ski jumpers; in grand fir, they lie to the sides, as if neatly combed. On branches that bear cones, the needles are upswept and pointed.

High-elevation tree. Like noble fir, this species is common at middle and high elevations of the Cascades from southern British Columbia to northern California; it occurs sparsely in the higher Coast Range elevations from central Oregon north. However, it grows farther north into British Columbia than does noble fir. In the high Cascades, Pacific silver fir and noble fir often grow together.

Tolerant of shade. In all stages of its life, Pacific silver fir is very tolerant of shade. For that reason, it commonly occurs in late successional forests. Seedlings can remain in the understory for many, many years, barely growing in height; then when the canopy opens, they can spring to life and grow rapidly.

Fire and regeneration. Pacific silver fir is quite sensitive to fire and its trees are often damaged or killed. But its cones commonly shed seeds following fires, helping reseed high elevation burned areas.

Bark of a young Pacific silver fir

Subalpine fir *Abies lasiocarpa*

Spire-like crown. Subalpine fir has the most arresting shape of any tree in the West. You wonder how any tree can have such a fragile, spire-like crown in such a harsh alpine environment. Branches near the top are very short and stiff, both to shed snow and to cut wind resistance. It reminds some of the Eiffel tower and others of a church spire.

Purple cones and uniform needles

Grows at tree line. Subalpine fir knows how to "hit the high spots" — it is rarely found below 3,000 feet in the Northwest. It grows abundantly in the Cascades and in the Blue Mountains, sparingly in the Siskiyous, and not at all in the Coast Range of Oregon; it can also be found in the Olympic Mountains of Washington, and at high elevations throughout British Columbia. Near timberline, subalpine fir commonly becomes dwarfed and contorted. On windy ridges it often forms "skirts" where the lower branches are protected under the snow from the shearing force of wind-blown ice and sand. These skirts provide homes for young trees and protection from the elements for birds and small mammals; in these groupings, the mother tree is always the tallest while the size and age of her children get smaller and younger farther away from her protection.

SIZE: A small conifer; usually less than 100′ tall and 2′ in diameter.

NEEDLES: White lines both above and below the needle; massed on the upper surface of the twig; very neat in appearance.

FRUIT: Cylindrical, woody cones about 2–4″ long; purple. Fall apart at maturity.

TWIGS: Terminal buds are small, round, and covered with resin.

BARK: Gray; smooth or ridged. Contains resin pockets in inner bark.

Recognizing subalpine fir. Location is the best clue. In Oregon and Washington, subalpine fir can be found growing with almost any of the other true firs, especially near Crater Lake — and it's not always easy to tell them apart just by their foliage. However, subalpine fir typically grows to the highest elevation. Subalpine fir needles are white on both surfaces, massed on the upper side of the twig, and often very uniform in length, almost as if they had been manicured. Cones are typically bright purple and often contain large, crystal-clear resin drops where insects have bored into them. Subalpine fir is the only one of the true firs having tiny pockets of clear resin well within the thick bark. Owing to the rigors of its high homeland, subalpine fir usually is less than 100 feet tall.

A haven for wildlife. Thickets formed by its dense, stiff lower foliage are a refuge for deer, mountain goats and other wildlife. Squirrels feast on seeds from the large purple cones.

Disease threat. An insect from Europe, the balsam woolly aphid, defoliates and kills subalpine, Pacific silver, and grand firs. The insect puts a sucking tube into the bark to obtain food and at the same time injects a toxin that kills trees if the attack is heavy enough. Control options are limited, but scientists have recently found several insect enemies of the aphid to help reduce its numbers.

Subalpine fir with "skirt" of lower branches and young seedlings

White fir *Abies concolor* • Sometimes called *Abies lowiana*

Recognizing white fir. Deep within its native range, white fir is fairly easy to distinguish from other true firs. However, in Oregon, where it crosses with grand fir, it's often difficult to distinguish from grand fir. In its pure form, white fir has long (2- to 3-inch)

White fir cones

needles that are uniformly white on both the upper and lower surface. They turn up around the twig, resulting in a U-shaped

appearance. In Oregon, the needles are commonly shorter, have distinct (and often very short) white bands on the upper needle surface, and may be flat, V- or U-shaped around the twig. As a result, white fir and grand fir often are difficult to tell apart, especially when they hybridize and one parent comes from each species! As a result of the similarities between grand and white fir, foresters have taken to calling both of them "grandicolor" from a combination of their scientific names.

A large white fir

Where it grows. Oregon is the northernmost frontier for white fir, which is more at home in California and the central and southern Rockies. It's fairly common in southwest Oregon, especially around Crater and Klamath lakes. Stragglers may reach the Three Sisters area in the Cascades and scattered points in the Blue Mountains. Fire suppression is allowing white fir to invade drier sites than it naturally occupied, thereby expanding its range.

Uses. While still alive, white fir is attacked by a variety of insects and diseases that result in rot. Also, it is susceptible to frost cracking, again resulting in rot. Despite these problems, all of which result in losses at the mill, the wood is suitable for sawn products and plywood and especially for making paper. When in good shape and good size, it can be quite valuable.

White fir's whitish hue, dense foliage, and perfect pyramidal growth form make it a prized ornamental tree. Many nurseries market it under the name "concolor fir" in recognition of its scientific name. It's also highly prized for Christmas trees in many parts of the country.

Abies lowiana. Some taxonomists distinguish between white fir of the Rockies (*Abies concolor*) and white fir of the Sierra Nevada (*Abies lowiana*), while some consider them varieties of the same species. Visual differences between them are slight, so we will lump them together.

SIZE: Grows to 200' tall and 5' in diameter.

NEEDLES: White bloom on upper and lower surfaces; may be in distinct lines, uniformly distributed over the entire surface, or just on tips of needles.

FRUIT: Upright, cylindrical cone; 3–5" long; bracts shorter than scales. Cone turns brown as it ages and falls apart when mature.

TWIGS: Terminal buds are clustered and slightly pitchy. Young twigs are greenish.

BARK: Grayish; thick; furrowed. Inner bark has two distinct bands of color: reddish-brown and cream (like Douglas-fir).

The thick, corky bark of white fir

Distinguishing between true firs

Identifying true firs is often difficult, especially if all six species are a possibility. Fortunately, the task can be made simpler by breaking them into groups of two, in the following manner:

- Grand and Pacific silver fir needles are "green above" — that is, they do not have white bloom on the upper surface of their needles; the four other species of true firs have bluish-white bloom on both their upper and lower surfaces.

- Of the four that have bloom on both surfaces, noble and California red fir have needles that are shaped like hockey sticks — that is, they have a distinct elbow. The needles of other species may be gently curved, but they don't exhibit "elbows." In addition, the youngest twigs of noble and California red firs are distinctly reddish-brown, while the other two have greenish twigs.

- That leaves subalpine and white fir. They have bloom on both the upper and lower surface of their needles, like noble and California red fir. But their needles are not bent like hockey sticks. They may bend more gently upward.

Distinguishing grand fir from Pacific silver fir

Grand fir

Pacific silver fir

These are the only two Northwest true firs whose needles are entirely green on their top surface (no white bloom). However, grand fir needles are a shiny yellow-green, and silver fir needles are a dark, rich green. The needles of both tree species have two whitish bands on their undersides, although silver fir's bands have a silvery blue cast while grand fir's have a greenish cast. Grand fir needles are always two-ranked (although they may be flat or V-shaped). Silver fir needles are not two-ranked, as several rows of short needles run along the top of each twig, pointing toward the tip of the twig like tiny ski-jumpers.

Grand fir

Pacific silver fir

Distinguishing noble fir from California red fir

Noble fir

California red fir

Both species have bluish white bloom on both upper and lower leaf surfaces (as do subalpine fir and white fir); both have reddish brown twigs; and both have needles that resemble hockey sticks. How can we separate them? Cones are the best clue — cones of both species grow large and upright, but noble fir cones have distinctive, papery bracts that stick out between each scale; the cone bracts in California red fir cones are shorter than their scales, so they do not stick out. Also look carefully at the top surface of each needle — noble fir usually has a tiny groove running down the middle of the needle, while California red fir usually has a ridge. Remember that hybrids between the two species typically have mixed characteristics.

Noble fir

California red fir

Distinguishing subalpine fir from white fir

Subalpine fir

White fir

Although both species have greenish twigs and whitish bloom on both surfaces of their needles, there the similarity ends. Subalpine is a small tree of the subalpine region, while white fir is a large tree of middle elevations. Subalpine's needles are short, densely packed, and tightly clustered on the top side of the twig. White fir's needles are typically much longer, more widely spaced along the twig, and tend to be two-ranked (although they may be flat, V-shaped, or U-shaped).

Subalpine fir

White fir

Yews *Taxus*

Yew is a small genus of about eight species scattered across North America, Europe and Asia. Although it's grouped with the conifers because it has needle-like foliage, its fruit is not a cone at all. Instead, it's an aril — a large, single seed surrounded by a soft, fleshy, orange-to-bright red pulp. Although they look inviting, DON'T TASTE THEM. They are highly poisonous to humans. All parts of all yews contain a natural chemical called taxol that attacks and kills rapidly dividing cells in humans and some other mammals. (But some are unaffected and actually browse the plants and eat the fruits.) This ability to kill rapidly dividing cells makes it promising in the treatment of certain types of cancer, but also makes it dangerous to ingest.

Only one yew, Pacific yew, is native to the Northwest. However, English yew is commonly planted in lawns and gardens for ornamental purposes. Its fruits are also highly toxic to humans.

Pacific yew *Taxus brevifolia*

Understory tree. Pacific yew is an inconspicuous tree most commonly found in the dark shadows of towering Douglas-firs and western hemlocks. Typically, it's small — usually under 40 feet tall — and lacks a distinctive form, sending branches

Pacific yews bend to reach the light.

wherever there's enough light to support growth. It grows very slowly, taking hundreds of years to reach its full size. If growing conditions are ideal and the forest is undisturbed for a very long time, Pacific yews may reach 75 feet tall and several feet in diameter. Pacific yew is one of the few conifers that can sprout from its base if its top is killed or damaged.

Recognizing Pacific yew. Pacific yew needles have four distinct characteristics that help separate them from other Northwest conifers:

- They are always two-ranked (they grow in a single plane).

- Their leaf tips come to a distinct, but soft, point.

- Both sides of their needles are green (dark green above and lighter green below, but no white bloom).

- Their edges curl under.

SIZE: Small understory tree. Generally under 50' tall and 2' in diameter.

NEEDLES: About 1" long; dark green above and lighter green below (not white); pointed, but not sharp; leaf margins rolled under; needles lie in a single plane.

FRUIT: Small red "berry" (aril) with a single large seed. POISONOUS to humans and many mammals!

TWIGS: Thin; remain bright green for several years before turning brown. Few side branches.

BARK: Thin; scaly; reddish-purple under the gray, flaky outer bark.

Dark green foliage

Pacific yew bark, far left. At top right, a bright red "berry," called an aril. Only female trees produce arils. Image at bottom right shows unripe arils; note the naked seed.

Western hemlock and grand fir are often two-ranked, but their needles have blunt tips. Redwood is two-ranked and sharp-tipped but has two white bands on the undersides of its leaves, and its edges are not curled under. Of all the conifers, Pacific yew needles are the darkest green. Pacific yew's purple, scaly bark is another good clue to its identity.

Unique fruit. Yews are the only conifers that have bright red fleshy "berries," called arils, for their fruit. Birds love to eat arils, but they're highly poisonous to humans, and are especially dangerous to small children. All yews are dioecious — this means that male and female flowers are borne on separate plants. Yew trees are either male or female; only female trees bear the bright red arils, while the male trees produce pollen.

Cancer-fighting bark. The bark of Pacific yew is gray and scaly on the outside and reddish-purple on the inside. Over the past several decades, it has been found to contain a chemical called taxol. The tree manufactures taxol to protect itself from insects and disease, but scientists have found that taxol can help humans fight cancer and several other diseases.

Range. Pacific yew grows from Alaska into California and the northern Rockies. It likes shady dells, stream banks, and moist flats at medium and low elevations. Although it's widespread, it's seldom common. It grows in small groves and as scattered individuals, not in dense stands.

Uses. Heavy, tough yew wood is superb for tools requiring resilience, such as bows and canoe paddles. Yews of other lands once furnished bows for ancient armies. The wood has a pretty rose-red color, but the small supply limits commercial use. It's very durable in contact with the soil, so it is often used for fence posts. Woodworkers must be careful not to breathe the sawdust from yews, as it is also toxic.

The tree manufactures taxol to protect itself from insects and disease, but scientists have found that taxol can help humans fight cancer.

Fall colors at Bull Prairie on the Fremont-Winema National Forest near Paisley, Oregon.

PHOTO:
U.S. FOREST SERVICE

Native broadleaves settle into Northwest niches

Although broadleaved trees from all over the world can grow in Oregon and Washington, only about 35 species are native here — and about a dozen of these commonly grow as shrubs rather than as trees. Based on the structure of their flowers and fruit, these 35 species can be grouped into about 17 genera. So, though they're not as economically important as the conifers, the broadleaves are a more diverse group than our conifers.

Broadleaved trees play fairly specialized roles in Northwestern forests. In some cases, they're early successional species, occupying areas where ground has recently been disturbed by avalanche, flood or windthrow. In other cases, they're espccially adapted to hot, dry conditions, particularly where soils are shallow and moisture-holding capacities are low. Others are able to tolerate wet soils during the growing season, an especially valuable adaptation in the large valleys of western Oregon. So, despite the fact that no single broadleaved tree dominates any of the Northwest's forests, it should be clear that broadleaved trees are a vital part of our forests.

To learn to identify our native broadleaved trees, refer to the broadleaf key that begins on page 75. Although it may appear complex, it's easy to use if you make one decision at a time. To learn more about Northwestern forests, turn to "Northwest forests," page 138.

Key to common broadleaved trees of the Pacific Northwest

To use this key

1. Begin with a tree, or a section of branch with needles or leaves.

2. Start at the top. Read the two statements directly below the starting point.

3. Decide which of the two statements (or drawings) better describes the tree. Then read the two statements directly under that box and make the same type of decision.

4. Continue until you've identified a single group of trees (called a genus). Turn to the page indicated and read the descriptions of individual species within that genus.

5. If the species description matches the tree you're trying to identify — GREAT! If it doesn't match, go back to start and try again.

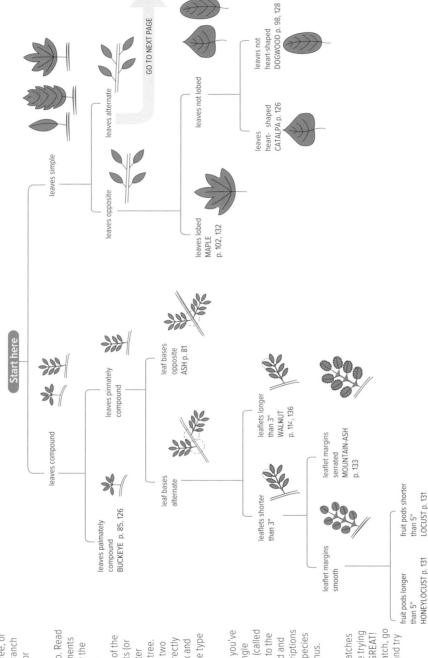

Start here

leaves compound

leaves simple

leaves palmately compound
BUCKEYE p. 85, 126

leaves pinnately compound

leaf bases alternate

leaf bases opposite
ASH p. 81

leaflets longer than 3"
WALNUT p. 114, 136

leaflets shorter than 3"

leaflet margins serrated
MOUNTAIN-ASH p. 133

leaflet margins smooth

fruit pods longer than 5"
HONEYLOCUST p. 131

fruit pods shorter than 5"
LOCUST p. 131

leaves opposite

leaves alternate

GO TO NEXT PAGE

leaves lobed
MAPLE p. 102, 132

leaves not lobed

leaves heart-shaped
CATALPA p. 126

leaves not heart-shaped
DOGWOOD p. 98, 128

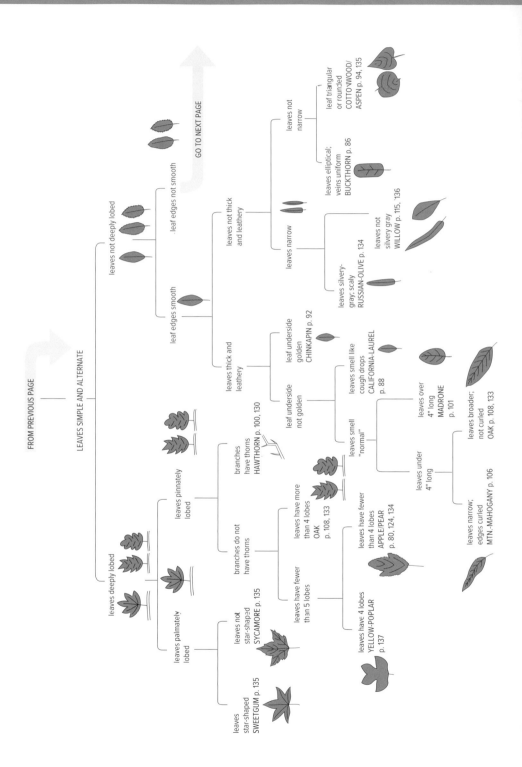

FROM PREVIOUS PAGE

LEAVES SIMPLE AND ALTERNATE

GO TO NEXT PAGE

leaves deeply lobed

leaves not deeply lobed

leaves palmately lobed

leaves pinnately lobed

leaf edges smooth

leaf edges not smooth

leaves star-shaped
SWEETGUM p. 135

leaves not star-shaped
SYCAMORE p. 135

branches have thorns
HAWTHORN p. 100, 130

branches do not have thorns

leaves thick and leathery

leaves not thick and leathery

leaves have more than 4 lobes
OAK p. 108, 133

leaves have fewer than 5 lobes

leaf underside golden
CHINKAPIN p. 92

leaf underside not golden

leaves narrow

leaves not narrow

leaves have fewer than 4 lobes
APPLE/PEAR p. 80, 124, 134

leaves have 4 lobes
YELLOW-POPLAR p. 137

leaves smell like cough drops
CALIFORNIA-LAUREL p. 88

leaves smell "normal"

leaves silvery-gray; scaly
RUSSIAN-OLIVE p. 134

leaves not silvery gray
WILLOW p. 115, 136

leaves elliptical; veins uniform
BUCKTHORN p. 86

leaf triangular or rounded
COTTONWOOD/ ASPEN p. 94, 135

leaves over 4" long
MADRONE p. 101

leaves under 4" long

leaves broader; not curled
OAK p. 108, 133

leaves narrow; edges curled
MTN.-MAHOGANY p. 106

FROM PREVIOUS PAGE

LEAVES SIMPLE, ALTERNATE, NOT LOBED AND MARGINS NOT SMOOTH

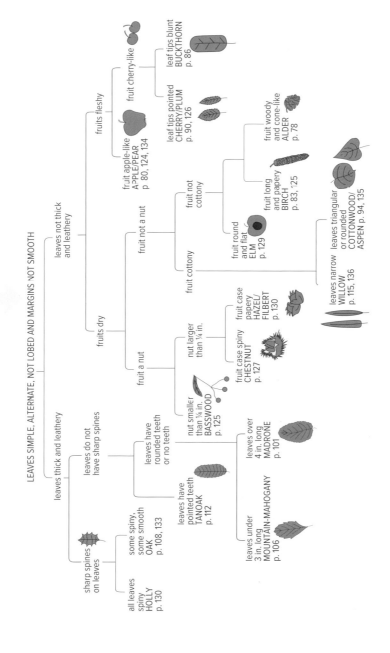

leaves thick and leathery

sharp spines on leaves

all leaves spiny
HOLLY
p. 130

some spiny, some smooth
OAK
p. 108, 133

leaves do not have sharp spines

leaves have pointed teeth
TANOAK
p. 112

leaves have rounded teeth or no teeth

leaves not thick and leathery

fruits dry

fruits fleshy

fruit apple-like
APPLE/PEAR
p 80, 124, 134

fruit cherry-like

leaf tips pointed
CHERRY/PLUM
p. 90, 126

leaf tips blunt
BUCKTHORN
p. 86

fruit a nut

nut smaller than ¼ in.
BASSWOOD
p. 125

nut larger than ¼ in.

fruit case spiny
CHESTNUT
p. 127

fruit case papery
HAZEL/FILBERT
p. 130

fruit not a nut

fruit cottony

leaves narrow
WILLOW
p. 115, 136

leaves triangular or rounded
COTTONWOOD/ASPEN p. 94, 135

fruit not cottony

fruit round and flat
ELM
p. 129

fruit long and papery
BIRCH
p. 83, '25

fruit woody and cone-like
ALDER
p. 78

leaves under 3 in. long
MOUNTAIN-MAHOGANY
p. 106

leaves over 4 in. long
MADRONE
p. 101

Red alder grows in dense, dark stands, reaching a height of 130 feet.

Alders *Alnus*

Alders like moist surroundings, and there are few creeks in western Oregon and Washington not overhung by them. Their peculiar woody cones (called strobiles) identify alders as surely as flat tails identify beavers. These strobiles hang from the trees throughout winter, like miniature lanterns. Alders shed their leaves while still green, which returns many nutrients directly to the soil. Also, alder roots contain bacteria-filled nodules that capture nitrogen from the air for the tree's use; when these roots die, the nitrogen is returned to the soil, greatly enhancing soil productivity.

Eight species of alder are native to North America. The Northwest has four: red, white, Sitka and thinleaf. Only the first two species commonly reach tree size, and only red alder is abundant. Knowing their ranges and leaf traits helps in separating one species from another.

Large alder trees

80 to 100 feet tall; single trunk

RED ALDER: Look for large, egg-shaped leaves whose margins are tightly rolled under (revolute), leaving a green rim around the underside of each leaf.

WHITE ALDER: Their leaves are large and egg-shaped, but the margins are NOT rolled under.

Alder shrubs or small trees

Usually under 25 feet tall; commonly with multiple trunks

SITKA ALDER: Leaf margins have a single row of very fine teeth; margins are not rolled under. (This tree will not be described further because it's primarily shrubby).

THINLEAF ALDER: Leaf margins have a double set of coarse teeth; margins are not rolled under. (This tree will not be described further because it's primarily shrubby).

Red alder leaves are double-toothed, and the edges tightly roll under. Its fruits resemble small pine cones, lasting through the winter.

Red alder *Alnus rubra*

Most common broadleaf. Red alder is the most common broadleaved tree in western Oregon and Washington, and is our most important hardwood by almost any standard. It likes cool, moist environments and is ever present in coastal forests, where it grows in dense, dark stands. Red alder is an aggressive seeder and a fast grower that reaches 130 feet tall. It's rare east of the Cascades and on the floor of the major valleys of western Oregon. (Most valley alders are white alders.)

Unique leaves. To identify red alder, look at its leaves and bark. The leaves are large and egg-shaped. Their edges are coarsely and bluntly double-toothed (each large tooth has several smaller teeth on it). Also, the edges are tightly rolled under (revolute), creating a distinct, green rim on the underside of each leaf.

The trunk of red alder is covered with gray-white bark with black patches. It looks like a white post that a child with muddy hands and feet tried to climb. Tiny, scalelike lichens growing on the bark add to its whiteness. Young trees have greenish bark because the lichens are not yet growing on it.

Where red alder gets its name. The sapwood of red alder takes on a reddish stain when freshly cut. Northwest Indian children used to play sick by chewing the inner bark, because the juice makes saliva as red as blood. Rubra, the scientific name for this species, is Latin for red.

Bright future. Although red alder is not a particularly large tree, it's a potentially important economic resource because of its fast growth and the large area of land it occupies. Large, straight logs are valued for cabinets, furniture and pallet lumber. Small and crooked logs are used for toys, novelties, firewood and pulp to make paper and composition boards. Red alder also is commonly planted in Douglas-fir forests to help sites recover from root rots and to help fertilize the site (because bacteria in their roots capture nitrogen from the air and make it usable for plants). A great deal of research is underway to find more uses for this underutilized species.

SIZE: Grows to 120' tall and 3' in diameter.

LEAVES: Simple, alternate and deciduous. Egg-shaped; 3–6" long. Margins doubly serrated and tightly rolled under. Veins very straight.

FRUIT: Small, brown, woody "cones" about 1" long.

TWIGS: Young twigs are triangular in cross-section. Buds are borne on short stalks.

BARK: Smooth, gray, and blotchy. Inner bark turns red when exposed to air.

Red male catkins shed millions of pollen grains each spring.

White alder *Alnus rhombifolia*

Where it grows. White alder is found on both sides of the Cascades, especially along streams. It's the alder most commonly found on the floor of the Willamette Valley, but it frequently mixes with red alder in the Umpqua and Rogue valleys. White alder grows from British Columbia through much of California and eastward into Idaho and Montana.

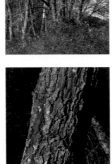

The bark of white alder is whitish when young, but turns dark as it ages.

White alder leaves have a single row of teeth along their edges. Margins are not rolled under.

Distinguishing it from red alder. White alder looks very much like red alder, but three differences help separate them. First, white alder leaves typically have a single row of teeth along their edges; red alder leaves have a double row. However, some white alder leaves have wavy edges and may appear to be doubly serrate, so look carefully. Second, white alder leaves do not have revolute margins — that is, their upper surface is not rolled under. Third, white alder's bark near the ground is platy and scaly and dark gray to black, while red alder's bark is smooth and splotchy white.

Uses. White alder grows too sparsely in the Northwest to be commercially important, but it does capture nitrogen, recycle nutrients, and drop leafy food into streams.

SIZE: Grows to 80' tall and 2' in diameter.

LEAVES: Simple, alternate, and deciduous. Egg-shaped; 2–4" long. Margins serrated or doubly serrated; not rolled under. Veins straight.

FRUIT: Small, brown, woody "cones" about 1" long.

TWIGS: Have stalked buds.

BARK: Gray and splotchy; breaks into scaly ridges.

Male catkins are not red like red alder, but still shed millions of pollen grains.

Apples and crab apples *Malus*

Although apples and pears are sometimes grouped in the same genus because their fruits are similar, newer classifications categorize apples as *Malus* and pears as *Pyrus*. Crab apples, which are simply small, often bitter-tasting apples, are included in *Malus*. While apples are easy to recognize from their flowers and fruits, they're more difficult to recognize from just their leaves. Also, wild apples commonly have leaves that look different from their relatives in orchards and yards. Although apples are grown throughout the Northwest for both ornamental and commercial purposes, only one species is native to our forests: Oregon crab apple. The rest have been introduced.

Oregon crab apple bears small, sour fruits. Flowers look like typical apple blossoms. It can be difficult to distinguish from black hawthorn.

Oregon crab apple *Malus fusca*

Formerly classified as *Pyrus fusca*

Wild apples. Cultivated apples are developed from small, bushy trees known as crab apples because of their tart taste. Oregon crab apple grows primarily west of the Cascade crest. It's especially common in coastal thickets, and it likes fence rows and forest edges, where birds drop its seeds. It's also called western and Pacific crab apple.

Similar to hawthorn. Oregon crab apple would be a snap to identify except for black hawthorn. They look alike, but black hawthorn has distinctive thorns and western crab apple doesn't (though some branch tips are nearly as sharp as thorns). Crab apple leaves may be either unlobed and serrated, or irregularly lobed and serrated — but the lobes are more sharply pointed than in black hawthorn, and usually there are only three (hawthorn has many). Oregon crab apple has ½-inch-long yellow to red fruits that are edible but sour. The flowers look like typical apple blossoms — small, white flowers in clusters.

Ashes *Fraxinus*

Ashes are easy to identify because they're one of the few groups of trees whose leaves are both opposite and pinnately compound — that is, there is a single leaf stalk with multiple leaflets arising along a long central stalk; and pairs of these sets of leaves arise oppositely from one another on the branch. If that is not enough, check their fruit. They have dry, single-winged seeds (samaras) that are shaped like canoes. Some say it's because ashes grow near water and their seeds are designed for floating. About 70 species of ash grow in the world; 16 are

SIZE: Small trees that grow to 40', or large shrubs, often growing in thickets.

LEAVES: Simple, alternate, deciduous. Egg-shaped; 1–4" long; margins serrated or irregularly lobed and serrated.

FRUIT: Small apples (about ½" in diameter); yellow to red.

TWIGS: Reddish-brown; spur shoots on older branches; no thorns (although some branch tips may be sharp).

native to North America. Only one is native to the Northwest, though many others are planted as ornamentals, especially for their bright yellow to red fall foliage.

Oregon ash
Fraxinus latifolia

Unique leaves. Oregon ash leaves are pinnately compound and oppositely arranged on their twigs. These two features occur together in no other native Northwest tree, although they do occur together in elderberry, a large shrub. Oregon ash's pinnately compound leaves have from five to nine leaflets per leaf; each leaflet is broadly elliptical in shape. In addition, the compound leaves arise from opposite sides of the twigs. This opposite nature can be easily determined in any season — from the leaves in summer and from the buds, leaf scars and twigs in winter.

Fruit, bark and location. An easy way to identify Oregon ash is by its fruits, which are dry, single-winged samaras. Each seed and wing combination is shaped like a canoe. Ash bark is crisscrossed with ridges and resembles a woven net. Oregon ash, a medium-size tree, is seldom taller than 80 feet. It likes the plentiful moisture of stream banks, sloughs and rich lowlands, and is able to survive in heavy clay bottomlands that drain poorly and stay wet for months.

An athlete's wood. Ash has many uses in sports — baseball bats, oars, skis and many other kinds of wooden sporting goods are made from ash trees native to eastern North America. Oregon ash has a similar-quality wood — hard and tough with beautiful grain and color — but it's used much less because of its limited availability. However, from time to time it's in strong commercial demand at attractive prices. Look at an ax handle or a wooden baseball bat and notice the wide wood rings. Wide rings indicate rapid growth when the tree was young. Ash wood of this sort is stronger than that from narrow-ring wood and is preferred for the manufacture of sports equipment and tool handles.

The compound leaves of Oregon ash arise from opposite sides of the twigs, and bark is marked by shallow ridges.

SIZE: Grows to 80′ tall and 3′ in diameter.

LEAVES: Pinnately compound (5–9 per leaf), opposite, deciduous. Leaflets are roughly elliptical with smooth or very slightly serrated margins.

FRUIT: Single samaras that hang in clusters. Shaped like a canoe.

TWIGS: Opposite twigs and buds. Stout.

BARK: Up to 2" thick; grayish-brown; flattened ridges.

Birches
Betula

Birches are easily recognized by their paperlike bark with distinctive horizontal markings called lenticels. In most species, the bark peels off in thin, papery strips. Another distinctive feature of all birches is their fruit — a papery, disintegrating, cylindrical cone about 1 inch long. Birches are common ornamental trees. There are about 50 species of birch in the world. Eight

Many Native Americans made canoes from strips of paper birch bark.

species reach tree size in North America, and two of these grow in the Pacific Northwest, though their ranges are small and scattered.

- **Paper birch:** bright white bark.
- **Water or red birch:** reddish-brown to black bark.

Paper birch
Betula papyrifera

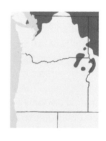

Unique bark. Bark is the most distinctive feature of paper birch. Although other birches may have whitish bark, none is as pure or peels as easily as that of

The leaves of paper birch are doubly serrate and feature long, tapering tips.

paper birch. In fact, its very name suggests this feature. Other paper birch features are elongated cone-like fruits that disintegrate when the seeds are mature (some say they resemble caterpillars), and doubly serrate leaves with long, tapering tips.

Canoe birch. Although Northwest Indians made their canoes from hollowed-out western redcedar logs, Indigenous People of Canada and the northern United States made theirs from birch bark — peeled in long strips and held together by rawhide laces and sticky, tarlike tree

SIZE: Grows to 70′ tall and 2′ in diameter.

LEAVES: Simple, alternate, deciduous. Egg-shaped; 2–4″ long; margins doubly serrate.

FRUIT: Tiny, winged nuts borne in a disintegrating cone about 1″ long.

TWIGS: Slender and droopy.

BARK: White and peeling in horizontal strips. Covered with large, horizontal fissures (called lenticels).

sap. These canoes carried Native Americans and early pioneers and adventurers across the continent from the Atlantic to the Rockies. Now, paper birch is used for veneer, pulpwood and novelties. It's also a common ornamental and shade tree because of its unique bark and graceful appearance.

Paper birch bears long, cone-like fruits

Range. Paper birch is one of North America's most widespread trees. It grows all across Canada and the northernmost portions of the United States. It occurs in eastern Washington and just touches the northeast corner of Oregon, where it grows sparingly in the Wallowa Mountains. Many white-barked birches are planted as ornamentals in the Pacific Northwest, but most are native to Europe and Asia and are not paper birch. Unfortunately, most birches are susceptible to a wood-boring beetle whose infestations often kill their host.

Water birch
Betula occidentalis

An apt name. Water birch is common along streams and on mountain slopes east of the Cascade crest. It grows most often in clusters 15 to 20 feet tall but may be taller on moist mountain sites.

The rounded leaves of water birch have coarse teeth, and its bark is reddish brown.

Caterpillar fruits.
The fruits of birches — thin, narrow "cones" made of papery scales — remind many people of fuzzy caterpillars. Water birch is no exception. Birch fruits fall apart while still hanging from the tree, scattering tiny, winged nutlets far and wide. The seeds are tiny and contain little stored energy, so they need to fall on moist, bare mineral soil if they are to survive.

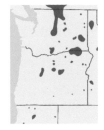

Also called red birch. Paper birch is noted for its bright white bark; the bark of water birch is reddish brown or coppery. As a result, it's sometimes called red birch. The leaves of water birch are rounder than those of paper birch and have coarser teeth, resembling the blade of an electric saw. Its twigs are slender and droopy like those of white birch, but they're covered with glistening drops of resin.

Water birch cones are made of papery scales that scatter when they fall.

SIZE: May grow as a shrub or small tree up to 30' tall.

LEAVES: Simple, alternate, deciduous. Roundish; 1–2" wide; coarsely serrated; often sticky.

FRUIT: Elongated papery cones that disintegrate at maturity. Tiny, winged seeds.

TWIGS: Slender, droopy and covered with sticky dots of resin.

BARK: Thin, reddish-brown to coppery; may curl but does not peel.

Buckeyes or horse-chestnuts

Aesculus

Members of the genus *Aesculus* are called buckeyes in the New World and horse-chestnuts in the Old World. Horse-chestnut is properly hyphenated to indicate that it's not a member of the true chestnut genus (*Castanea*). In Great Britain they are sometimes called conkers because their seeds are used to play a game of the same name. There are 12 to 15 species of *Aesculus* growing worldwide, all in temperate regions of the Northern Hemisphere. Six or seven species are native to North America with about the same number in Eurasia. They are all noted for large, palmately compound leaves (like fingers radiating out from the palm of a hand), very large and showy spikes of flowers, and large, round, leathery capsules bearing several large seeds, with each seed bearing a large, white circular scar. Unlike the edible seeds of true chestnuts, the seeds of *Aesculus* are toxic to humans and domestic animals.

California buckeye is rare in the Northwest.

SIZE: Grows to 40 feet tall in CA but less in OR; often has multiple trunks.

LEAVES: Palmately compound, with 5 leaflets, opposite, and deciduous. Leaflets commonly 3–7" long

FRUIT: Large yellow-brown capsule; pear- or fig shaped. 2–4" long. Typically 3 large red-brown seeds with one large white dot on each seed. Seeds are poisonous.

TWIGS: Buds and branchlets are opposite. Terminal buds are large and sticky.

BARK: Smooth and gray.

California buckeye *Aesculus californica*

Rare in the Northwest. California buckeye grows almost exclusively in the foothills of the Coastal Ranges and Sierra Nevadas of California, where it is fairly common. Many maps don't show it extending into the Pacific Northwest, but there is at least one small population in southwestern Oregon, near Gold Hill. It is so rare that it didn't even appear in the botanical literature of Oregon until around 1970, although, with additional searching, stumps have been found as old

Leathery capsules bear large seeds that are toxic.

as 250 years. In fact, its history in Oregon may be much older than that, as it may have marched northward from California with other chaparral associates several thousand years ago, near the end of the last glacial period. Most buckeye trees in Oregon have already been lost to firewood cutting, cattle grazing, agriculture and land development. As a result, their future in Oregon is in question unless specific steps are taken to preserve them.

How to identify it. California buckeye is easy to identify because of its large palmately compound leaves that arise opposite one another from the twigs, and large, showy spikes of pinkish white flowers. Its fruits are large, brown, pear- or fig-shaped capsules, usually bearing three large reddish-brown seeds inside; each seed has a large white hilar fissure on it (the spot where the seed was connected to the parent plant). Seeds (and all parts of the plant) are mildly toxic to humans and livestock. California buckeye grows as a small tree or large, spreading shrub with smooth, gray bark.

Adapted to the chaparral. California buckeye is well adapted to the hot, dry conditions (Mediterranean climate) found in the chaparral of California. Its leaves are among the first to emerge in the spring, but may stop photosynthesizing in the driest part of the year and leave that task to chlorophyll found in the bark and seed pods.

Identify California buckeye by its compound leaves and showy flowers.

Buckthorns *Rhamnus*
Sometimes classified as *Frangula*

This group of small trees and shrubs has many members — almost 100 worldwide. Only five reach tree size in North America, and only one of those occurs in Northwest forests. We do, however, have several species that typically grow as shrubs. Many of the buckthorns have thorns, but some do not. These are the shrubs that will not be described further:

Cascara buckthorn reaches 20 to 40 feet tall in moist shade.

- **Alderleaf buckthorn *(Rhamnus alnifolia):*** A spreading shrub that reaches 6 feet tall. Widespread in the U.S. and Canada, but in the Northwest occurs only in southwest and northeast Oregon and northeast Washington.
- **Coffeeberry *(Rhamnus californica):*** An upright evergreen shrub that reaches 6 to 10 feet tall. Grows from southwestern Oregon through California.
- **Hollyleaf redberry *(Rhamnus illicifolia):*** A rambling shrub that reaches 10 to 12 feet tall. Grows across western North America but is especially common in foothills and chaparral of California.
- **Red buckthorn *(Rhamnus rubra):*** A spreading shrub that reaches 6 feet tall. Grows primarily in California but does occur in southwestern Oregon.

Cascara buckthorn *Rhamnus purshiana*

Sometimes classified as *Frangula purshiana*

Cascara = bark. "Cascara" means "bark" in Spanish. The name probably came from early Spanish explorers who learned of the medicinal properties of cascara bark from California Indians. Cascara bark contains a powerful drug used to make laxatives and tonics. The entire world's supply comes from the Pacific Northwest. Synthetic compounds have reduced the demand for bark a bit, but cascara is used in so many drugs all over the world that a steady future demand is predicted. A tree 6 inches in diameter

Clues to identifying cascara buckthorn (clockwise from top left): buds exposed to the weather; chalky bark; ridges on the underside of leaves; and fruits attractive to wildlife.

will produce 12 to 15 pounds of dry bark — enough to furnish one dose each to more than 2,000 people.

Naked buds. One detail will positively identify cascara buckthorn — naked winter buds. Other tree buds have an armor of close-fitting scales, but cascara's buds are shielded from winter weather only by a fuzz of rusty brown hairs. The oblong leaves are also distinctive — their veins stick out like ribs, especially on the underside. Cascara buckthorn has a smooth, gray bark resembling young alder, but it is often embellished with chalky white lines and patches. So, cascara is a cinch to recognize: ribbed leaves in summer, naked buds during winter, and gray, splotchy bark throughout the year. While many buckthorns are armed with thorns (hence the name) cascara buckthorn is not.

Other uses. Grouse, raccoons and other wildlife often take the cherrylike fruits before we see them. Green or red at first, they ripen to a blue-black. The hard seed inside is not digested, so birds scatter them beside roads and fields and along fence rows. The fruits contain the same chemical as the bark, so generally humans don't eat them.

SIZE: Grows as a small tree (to 50' tall and 2' in diameter) or an erect shrub (to 15' tall) with multiple stems.

LEAVES: Simple, alternate, deciduous. Oblong to elliptical; 2–6" long; smooth, wavy, or finely serrated edges. Prominent, straight veins.

FRUIT: Black, cherrylike fruit, ¼–½" in diameter. Inedible and causes diarrhea.

TWIGS: Naked winter buds. Tiny, brown, hairy leaves folded around smaller leaves.

BARK: Thin and grayish with chalky, white patches.

Understory tree. Cascara buckthorn likes moist locations and deep shade. It mixes with the maples and red alder west of the Cascade crest and reaches a height of 20 to 40 feet with abundant moisture — if it escapes the bark peelers. Cascara has a short trunk that divides into numerous branches to form a rounded head.

Cascara conservation. Cascara buckthorn sprouts vigorously when its top is cut or injured — as long as the entire trunk is not peeled. Therefore, bark peelers will perpetuate their business by cutting down the tree before stripping it, so the stump is not peeled.

California-laurel is also called Oregon-myrtle, bay-laurel and pepperwood. Its wood is typically called myrtlewood.

California-laurel *Umbellularia*

California-laurel is truly unique in the plant world. The genus has only one species, so genus and species have the same common name: California-laurel. The world's only California-laurel grows along the coast of California and southwestern Oregon. In Oregon, it's commonly called Oregon-myrtle, while in California it's also called bay, California bay, bay laurel, and pepperwood — names that refer to the spicy aroma and taste of its leaves. Regardless of the name used for the tree, the wood typically is called myrtlewood. The hyphens in the common names help us remember that this tree is neither a laurel nor a myrtle — it is its own classification.

California-laurel *Umbellularia californica*

Often called Oregon-myrtle

Easy to identify. California-laurel is marked by two unique characteristics: the pungent odor of its leaves and its olive-like fruit. When bruised, its evergreen leaves give off a powerful scent of

SIZE: Grows to 100' tall and 5' in diameter. Often has multiple stems and a ball-shaped crown.

LEAVES: Simple, alternate, evergreen. Pungent odor when crushed. Elliptical to lanceolate; 2–6" long and 1" wide; smooth margins; dark green above and paler green below.

FRUIT: Size and shape of a large olive; purple with yellow stalk when ripe; single large seed.

BARK: Smooth and gray-brown when young. Thin, reddish-brown, and scaly when mature.

camphor, the same smell used in many cough drops and medicated jellies. If inhaled deeply, it pains the sinuses, and if rubbed in the eyes it stings for hours. To overcome chill, Hudson's Bay Company trappers made a tea from the leaves of California-laurel. The fruit of California-laurel is the size and consistency of a large, ripe olive. It has a single large seed and an outer covering that ranges from purple to black when ripe. The fruit is

California-laurel fruit, top left, turns purple to black when ripe. The tree commonly grows multiple stems. Its dark, shiny leaves have been used to make tea.

connected to the twig by a stem that looks like a yellow golf tee. All-in-all, a colorful combination.

When in Oregon. California-laurel is commonly known in Oregon as Oregon-myrtle, or myrtlewood. When grown in the open, it resembles a big pincushion. Its evergreen leaves are shiny and glint brightly in the sun. California-laurel trees often grow in dense, multistemmed clumps, from which two or three trunks will assume dominance and perhaps grow fairly straight in closed stands. On moist bottomlands, heights of 150 feet and diameters of 5 feet are possible, but on average sites, trees are 40 to 80 feet tall. On harsh sites, they may even grow as tangled shrubs. A superb grove of these trees grows at Loeb State Park near Brookings, Oregon. California-laurel grows throughout California, in all but its driest regions. It is not native to Washington.

Famous wood. California-laurel wood is marvelous for carving and turning. It is beautiful, is easily worked with tools, and polishes like marble. Dozens of small woodworking shops in southwestern Oregon and California turn out bowls, clocks, book-ends, and other products with its wood. In machining qualities, the wood equals the very best American hardwoods and is in demand for furniture, cabinets, paneling, veneer and gun stocks. Finished myrtlewood is the highest priced of native western hardwoods. The 1869 celebration that marked completion of the first transcontinental railroad tells us something about the fame of this distinctive wood. The gold spikes were driven into a handsome railroad tie of polished myrtlewood.

California-laurel wood is marvelous for carving and turning. The wood equals the very best American hardwoods and is in demand for furniture, cabinets, paneling, veneer and gun stocks. Finished myrtlewood is the highest priced of native western hardwoods.

Cherries and plums *Prunus*

Bitter cherry grows in most western states.

Cherry and plum trees belong to a genus that includes apricot, peach, nectarine and almond trees. Collectively, they're called "stone fruits" because they have fleshy fruits with a single, large seed inside. Two other distinctive features of *Prunus* include small glands on the base of the leaf or on the petiole (leaf stalk), and stipules — small, leafy "ears" that appear where the petiole joins the twig. North America contains approximately 30 species of this genus, but only three are native to the Northwest — two cherries and one plum. It's not uncommon, however, for domesticated cherry trees to "escape" from farms and yards and to find a home in our woods.

Native *Prunus*

BITTER CHERRY *(Prunus emarginata)*: Leaves are elliptical; flowers grow in round clusters; fruits are bright red; bases of leaves often have tiny glands (raised bumps).

COMMON CHOKECHERRY *(Prunus virginiana)*: Leaves are oblong to obovate; flowers grow in elongated clusters; petioles often have distinct glands. Fruits range from red to dark purple.

KLAMATH PLUM *(Prunus subcordata)*: Leaves are ovate to oval; flowers grow in round clusters; leaf bases or petioles often have small glands. Fruits range from yellow to purple. Short branches, called spur shoots, are often as pointed as thorns.

Non-native *Prunus*

CHERRY PLUM *(Prunus cerasifera)*: Native to southeastern Europe and western Asia, but widely naturalized elsewhere. Bark is reddish-brown to dark gray and furrows with age. Leaves are green to purple. Fruits are up to 1 inch in diameter; yellow to red; and range from sweet to bland.

SWEET CHERRY *(Prunus avium)*: Native to Europe and Asia Minor. Smooth, reddish-brown bark with prominent horizontal lenticels, often peeling in horizontal stripes. Egg-shaped leaves are larger than native cherries (3 to 6 inches long); typically with two to five prominent red glands on the petiole. Fruits are red to very dark red and tasty. Widespread in Oregon and Washington.

Bitter cherry *Prunus emarginata*

Tiny glands at the base of leaves

Bitter fruit. Most of us relish the sweet taste of commercial cherries, but the bright red fruit of bitter cherries makes us squint and pucker. For this reason, they are considered inedible. The leaves of bitter cherry are narrower than those of most cherries, and their tiny glands are borne on the base of their leaves rather than on their petioles. Their small, white flowers are borne in small, rounded

Cluster of flowers

SIZE: Grows to 50' tall and 18" in diameter.

FRUIT: Small, bright red, juicy fruit with a single large seed.

LEAVES: Simple, alternate. Elliptical; 1–3" long. Glands on base of leaves.

TWIGS: Slender; reddish-brown. Spur shoots common.

BARK: Thin; reddish-brown; tends to break and curl horizontally. Large horizontal lenticels on bark.

Bright red fruits are bitter; reddish bark has prominent lenticels.

clusters. Their reddish-brown bark has large, horizontal pores (called lenticels) that tend to break and curl around the tree.

Uses. Deer and elk browse the leaves and twigs, and many birds and mammals delight in the ripened fruit. When the tree grows large enough, its wood is valuable for furniture and gun stocks.

Range. Bitter cherry grows on moist sites throughout most of the western states. It is widespread in Oregon and Washington.

Chokecherry *Prunus virginiana*

Shrubby. Chokecherry is most commonly a shrub but also can grow as a small tree.

Fall foliage

Its leaves come in a variety of shapes but are generally egg-shaped to elliptical. Its leaf glands typically are on the petiole right below the leaf blade. Its small, white flowers are a good identifying characteristic because they grow in elongated clusters. Its ripe fruit ranges from red to dark purple. Its bark is thin and scaly but does not peel as readily as many other cherries, and lenticels are not evident.

Uses. Deer and elk browse its leaves and twigs. Birds and small mammals love its fruit — and so do humans, who gather it for jellies and wine. It's said that Sacajawea, the well-known Native American woman, was captured by another tribe while she was gathering chokecherries and was taken east, where Lewis and Clark later found her.

Chokecherry flowers and dark purple fruit

SIZE: Up to 30' tall.

FRUIT: Small, purple, juicy fruit with a single large seed.

LEAVES: Simple, alternate. Ovate to elliptical; 2–4" long. Glands usually on petiole.

TWIGS: Slender; reddish-brown; smooth. Spur shoots common.

BARK: Thin, broken; scaly. Lenticels not present.

Range. Grows throughout the West but also spans Canada and the northern United States. It is widespread in Oregon and Washington.

Klamath plum *Prunus subcordata*

Large fruit. Fruit is perhaps the feature that distinguishes Klamath plum from other native cherries and plums. Klamath plums are much larger than cherries (½ to 1 inch long) and are oblong; ripe plums range in color from yellow to purple. The leaves of Klamath plum are broadly ovate and have small greenish glands either on the petiole or on the base of the leaf. Its flowers are white and are borne in loose, roundish clusters. The bark may be scaly, but it does not peel like the bark of

Klamath plum grows individually or in thickets.

Spiny spur shoot

Egg-shaped leaves

Flowers

Edible fruit

many other cherry trees. Its many spur shoots resemble thorns, but they often have buds on them. The tree sprouts vigorously from underground stems called rhizomes and forms dense, spiny thickets.

Uses. Like its relatives, Klamath plum is browsed by large mammals, and its fruit is eaten by a variety of animals, including humans.

Range. Klamath plum likes drier climates than other members of its genus. It ranges from southern Oregon to central California.

SIZE: Shrub or small tree growing to 25′ tall.

FRUIT: Oblong; ½–1″ long; yellow, dark red, or purple.

LEAVES: Simple, alternate, deciduous. Ovate; about 1–3″ long. Glands on petioles or base of leaf.

TWIGS: Slender; reddish-brown; conspicuous lenticels. Spur shoots often sharp.

BARK: Grayish-brown; fissured and broken into plates; may be scaly; thin (¼″ thick).

Chinkapins *Chrysolepis*

Until recently, the chinkapins (chinquapin is an alternate spelling) of North America and eastern Asia were lumped into a single genus, *Castanopsis*. Now, the two species from North America are classified as *Chrysolepis*, while the 100+ species of eastern Asia retain the name *Castanopsis*.

Both species of North American chinkapins grow along the West Coast, are evergreen, have triangular nuts borne in spiny burrs, and have golden scales on the underside of their leaves. One grows as a large tree, and the other (*Chrysolepis sempervirens*) as a shrub at high elevations.

Golden chinkapin *Chrysolepis chrysophylla)*

Unique fruit. Golden chinkapin has a light brown, spiny burr that you will not confuse with the fruit of any other Northwestern tree. It resembles that of the true chestnuts of the eastern United States and Asia. Each burr contains one or two yellowish brown, triangular nuts that are good to eat. However, few humans know their taste, for they're guarded as well as if surrounded by porcupines. But chipmunks and squirrels know exactly how to gain entry.

Golden chinkapin can grow to 150 feet tall.

SIZE: Grows to 150' tall and 6' in diameter. Grows as a shrub at high elevations.

LEAVES: Simple, alternate, evergreen. Lanceolate; 2–5" long; stiff and leathery; green above and golden below; smooth margins.

FRUIT: Sharp, spiny burr with 1 or 2 triangular nuts.

TWIGS: Yellow, star-shaped pith. Terminal buds are clustered.

BARK: Deeply furrowed and ridged; 1–2" thick.

Helpful name. Golden chinkapin's name helps identify it because its leaves are golden underneath. It's so distinctive that you'll know it immediately when you see it, even for the first time. Its leaves are evergreen, leathery, 2 to 5 inches long, and tapered at both ends. Its

Chinkapin fruits are brown, triangular nuts held inside spiny burrs.

creamy white flowers continue to bloom throughout the summer and make the tree conspicuous, especially where it's shrubby and the flowers are near eye level. They're arranged in fluffy spikes that stick out stiffly in various directions like the pegs on a clothes tree. They emit a strong, musky smell that hangs in the air with the pervasiveness of a skunk's odor but is less objectionable. The scientific name of the species, *chrysophylla,* means "gold leaf."

Range. Golden chinkapin grows over most of western Oregon and northwestern California — mostly below 5,000 feet, and at scattered points on the east slopes of the Cascades. It does not grow into Washington. In northwest Oregon and in high country, it's a low shrub and frequently grows in thickets. From Benton County south, trees commonly grow to 100 feet tall and 4 feet in diameter. Looking like ornamentals, the shiny, dense pyramids of chinkapin

Golden chinkapin leaves are green on top, gold on the bottom. Bark is gray, and long, fluffy male flowers are loaded with pollen.

stand out on forested hills, especially in winter when many other broadleaves are bare. Forest-grown specimens on favorable sites tend to have straight trunks, rather like conifers.

Uses. Golden chinkapin has excellent qualities for furniture, hardwood plywood, construction lumber, and packaging. However, commercial use is limited by the scattered distribution of large trees and irregular growth of their trunks.

Cottonwoods, poplars and aspens *Populus*

Three names for the same genus: members of this group of trees may be called cottonwoods, poplars or aspens, depending on what species they are. Nonetheless, they're all members of the same genus, *Populus*. Perhaps the most distinguishing feature of this group of trees is their cottony fruits that fill the air and water around them in early spring. Because of this, male trees often are selected for shade and landscaping to avoid the unsightly "cotton" showered all over the place by female trees. The leaves of *Populus* tend to have silvery or white backsides and very long leaf stems, which make it apparent when the wind is blowing through them.

About a dozen members of this genus are native to North America. As a group, they're

Black poplars, like other members of *Populus*, are known for yellow fall colors.

fast growing, they sprout easily from root suckers and cut branch tips, and they turn bright yellow in fall. Trees within the genus can be crossed readily to form hybrids whose growth characteristics often far exceed either of their parents. As a result, many hybrids are grown in large plantations to produce wood fiber for paper.

Two species are native to Oregon and Washington and are widely distributed, but many others have been planted as ornamentals, as shade trees, and for wind breaks. Some have escaped cultivation and become naturalized (that is, they grow on their own).

Northwest natives

BLACK COTTONWOOD: Huge trees at maturity that may exceed 200 feet tall and 6 feet in diameter. Leaves are mostly large and triangular but may be spear-shaped; undersides are white with bronze stains.

QUAKING ASPEN: A moderate-sized tree at maturity, usually under 80 feet tall and 2 feet in diameter. Leaves may be heart-shaped or nearly round; undersides are pale green rather than white, as they are in many members of the genus. The leaf stems (called petioles) are flat in cross section, causing leaves to flutter in the wind. Bark is smooth and greenish white but does not peel like paper birch.

Non-native and less common *Populus*

These are not further described in this section, but some are described in "Common ornamental trees."

BLACK POPLAR *(Populus nigra):* Native to Eurasia; only one spot found in Oregon. Leaves triangular to diamond-shaped. Invasive.

EASTERN COTTONWOOD *(Populus deltoides):* Common from the Rockies to the Atlantic Ocean. Perhaps only one small population in eastern Oregon. Leaves are large and triangular with coarse teeth along their margins.

FREMONT'S COTTONWOOD *(Populus fremontii):* Native to California and the southwestern states; only one small spot of it found in Oregon. Heart-shaped leaves edged in coarse teeth.

WHITE POPLAR *(Populus alba):* Introduced from Eurasia but has escaped cultivation and is quite invasive. Leaves typically five-lobed with undersides covered in bright white scurfy down.

Black cottonwood *Populus trichocarpa*

Also called *Populus balsamifera*

Silvery flashes. Black cottonwood leaves come in two distinct shapes: triangular and spear-shaped. Spear-shaped leaves are most common on sprouts arising from roots or the base of the tree. Triangular leaves are more typical and dominate the tree's crown. Regardless of the leaves' shapes, their long and sometimes flat petioles cause them to flash their bronzy white undersides when stirred by the wind. The flashing that results can be used to identify cottonwoods from quite a distance. There is perfume all around when the long, shiny cottonwood buds open. They're coated with a sweet-smelling, sticky resin, sometimes called balsam, which is responsible for local names of "balm" or "bam."

Tallest broadleaf in western North America. The tall, broadleaved trees lining rivers west of the Cascade crest are usually black

You'll see tall black cottonwood along most rivers west of the Cascades.

  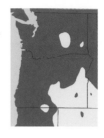

Black cottonwood fruits. Cotton puffs bear tiny seeds on the wind.

cottonwoods. Cottonwoods are the tallest, and often broadest, western broadleaved tree. Giants more than 9 feet thick and 200 feet tall once grew along the Columbia River flats. Black cottonwood is also a familiar tree along streams east of the Cascade crest.

Along the Oregon Trail. To pioneers on the old Oregon Trail, cottonwoods (a mix of species — black, eastern, narrowleaf, Fremont's) were extremely important. For nearly a thousand miles of their journey, cottonwoods were the only shade trees to be found. Cottonwoods still help make prairie farms and villages attractive. Although used a little for lumber and excelsior (packing material made of shaved wood before Styrofoam nurdles and plastic bubble wrap were invented), black cottonwood is always in demand for paper making. In fact, the earliest forest tree plantings in this region were black cottonwoods set out along the Willamette River near Oregon City in 1901 to supply a local pulp mill.

Range. Black cottonwood has a large but winding range. It stretches from southeast Alaska into Baja California and from the Pacific to the Dakotas. But for much of its range, it grows only along rivers and streams, avoiding hot, dry territory.

Quaking aspen *Populus tremuloides*

Maturing female catkin

Widespread. Although quaking aspen grows in more states than any other tree, it grows sparingly in the Northwest. It grows in our upper Cascades and eastward, especially along mountain streams, on moist slopes, in openings in the woods, and near the edges of mountain lakes and meadows. It also grows beneath pine forests bordering the high desert. Aspens are scarce in western Washington and Oregon, although a small population has been found in Benton County, Oregon, perhaps carried here in the Missoula floods some 13,000–15,000 years ago.

SIZE: Grows to 200' tall and 6' in diameter.

LEAVES: Simple, alternate, deciduous. Triangular; 3–6" long but sometimes much larger; green above and white below, often with rusty markings. Margins are smooth or with rounded teeth.

FRUIT: Round capsules on a string, each containing many tiny, cottony seeds.

TWIGS: Stout. Terminal buds are cigar-shaped, sticky and smelly.

BARK: Smooth and gray on young trees. Furrowed and ridged on mature trees.

Easy to learn. A beginner learns aspen almost without trying. The smooth, greenish-white bark has just enough chlorophyll to photosynthesize before the leaves come out in spring. But the leaf has a special feature that identifies aspen — a flat, flexible leaf stem held at right angles to the leaf blade. The slightest breath of wind sets the leaves dancing. The dainty aspen is conversational; its leaves whisper to the winds. Those same leaves daub the mountains with yellow gold in October. Small wonder it is a popular ornamental.

Quaking aspen spreads via underground root sprouts, often forming huge clones.

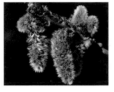

Male flowers, left, and the characteristic "eyes" that form around branches on the trunk.

SIZE: Small tree growing to 80' tall and 2' in diameter. Short lived.

LEAVES: Simple, alternate, deciduous. Ovate to round; 2–3" in diameter; green above and paler below; edges smooth or with rounded teeth. Petioles long and flat.

FRUIT: Cone-shaped capsule with cottony seeds.

BARK: Greenish-white when young. May turn dark and furrowed with age.

Disturbance-related species. Aspens are short-lived trees that sprout profusely from their roots, especially when they're injured. Fire plays an important role in maintaining aspen in the forest. When fires are free to burn, many aspens are damaged and send up new, vigorous sprouts. When fire is limited, individual trees soon die and are replaced by more shade-tolerant species. An original tree and its attached sprouts are called a clone; all members of the clone are genetically identical to one another. One clone in Colorado is reported to have 47,000 trees attached to the same root and may be the largest single organism in the world.

Important to wildlife. Though the inner bark of aspen is bitter to our taste, it's a favorite of beavers, who store cuttings for winter meals. Many other animals, including livestock, browse the bark, buds, and shoots. Because aspens sprout so easily from the roots, entire stands that have grown above the reach of wildlife can be disked into the ground by giant cutting blades in order to stimulate new growth.

Aspen, Colorado. The mountainsides of central Colorado are so famous for their beautiful stands of aspen that the town of Aspen adopted the tree's name.

Dogwoods *Cornus*

Dogwoods are noted for opposite leaves whose veins turn dramatically toward the apex when they reach the outer edge, and for large, showy flowers. Actually, the showy "petals" that comprise the flower are white or pink leaves, called bracts, that surround clusters of tiny, densely packed flowers. Of the 45 species of dogwood in the world, 13 are native to North America. Of these, only three species — one tree and two shrubs — are native to the Pacific Northwest, although many others have been introduced for ornamental purposes.

- **Brown dogwood *(Cornus glabrata):*** Native primarily to California but just crossing the border into southwestern Oregon. A large shrub, often forming dense thickets. Has clusters of many small, fuzzy-white flowers not surrounded by large bracts; followed by blueish-white berries. Bark is reddish-purple to brown. Typically grows near water. (Because it grows as a shrub, it will not be described further in this book.)

- **Pacific dogwood *(Cornus nuttallii):*** Grows as a tree; has large, showy, white "petals" surrounding each flower; branches typically dip between leaf clusters; fruits are orange to red berry-like drupes.

- **Western dogwood *(Cornus sericea):*** Grows only as a shrub; has clusters of many small, white flowers each with its own set of petals, rather than large, showy "petals" surrounding each clump of flowers; branches are straight; fruits are white; twigs are often bright red, giving rise to another common name, red-osier dogwood. (See *Shrubs to Know in Pacific Northwest Forests,* also published by OSU Extension.)

Pacific dogwood *Cornus nuttallii*

Unique flowers. No one mistakes Pacific dogwood during the flowering season because it has the most brilliant white blooms in our forests. Dogwood flowers are actually small and inconspicuous, but they're borne in a dense head surrounded by a set of large, white, petal-like leaves called bracts. Four to six of these showy leaves surround each buttonlike cluster of tiny, greenish-yellow flowers. From each cluster of flowers will arise several bright red "berries" to delight birds in fall and winter. Dogwood leaves, like its flowers, are nearly unmistakable. Their veins curve to follow the outline of the leaf — and they turn brilliant red in autumn. Pacific dogwood flowers most heavily in the spring but often has a second small bloom in fall.

Pacific dogwood flower and fruit

Understory tree. Dogwoods commonly grow 20 to 30 feet tall but may reach 50 feet or more. They can endure shade and grow quite large

SIZE: Grows to 60′ tall but usually much smaller.

LEAVES: Simple, opposite, deciduous. Ovate; 3–5″ long; smooth, wavy margins; curved veins. Turn bright red in autumn.

FLOWERS: Tiny, whitish flowers surrounded by 4 or 6 large, white bracts.

FRUIT: Flattened, reddish "berries" in dense clusters.

TWIGS: Both twigs and buds display an opposite arrangement. Branches are not straight, but dip from leaf cluster to leaf cluster.

BARK: Thin, gray, and smooth.

as understory trees in tall conifer forests west of the Cascades. Old dogwoods have bark that is broken into small, thin scales resembling alligator hide. Pacific dogwoods grow on the west side of the Cascades and Sierras from British Columbia to southern California; they also grow sporadically in wetter parts of Idaho.

Why dogwood? Skewers, or "dags," once were made from the wood of this tree, giving it the name "dagwood" that later became "dogwood." Pacific dogwood closely resembles the famed eastern dogwood, whose similar heavy, hard wood is used for textile shuttles, golf clubs, and piano keys. Botanist-explorer David Douglas thought Pacific dogwood was the eastern dogwood, but in 1835 Thomas Nuttall found differences in the floral leaves.

Color abounds. Find Pacific dogwood and you find color: white blossoms, clusters of bright red fruit, and fall foliage that runs from green to orange, red and purple. Dogwoods in bloom are considered by many our most beautiful trees. Nature essayist Ben Hur Lampman spoke of them as white sails on the hill slope. Pacific dogwoods are commonly planted as ornamental trees along our streets and in our yards. However, that practice is slowing as native dogwoods, in both forests and planted settings, are being killed by a rapidly spreading fungal disease called Anthracnose. Some species of Asian dogwoods appear resistant to this disease and are being planted instead of native species.

Dogwoods display a shower of brilliant white blooms in spring, and green leaves turn red in fall. The bark of old dogwoods is said to resemble the scales of an alligator hide.

Hawthorns *Crataegus*

Hawthorn is a large, diverse group of small trees and shrubs. Hundreds of species and varieties have been developed for ornamental planting. Two distinctive features of hawthorns are sharp, woody thorns and small, colorful, apple-like fruits. Hawthorns are often planted because of their beautiful flowers and colorful fruit.

Two species are native to Oregon, although others have been distributed far and wide by birds and humans. The Oregon natives are relatively easy to tell from each other when they have fruit but may be difficult at other times.

Black hawthorn

- **Black hawthorn:** Grows as a tree or shrub; black fruit; thorns usually shorter than 1 inch.

- **Columbia hawthorn:** Grows only as a shrub; red fruit; thorns usually longer than 1 inch; grows on east flank of Cascades and along the Columbia Gorge. (See *Shrubs to Know in Pacific Northwest Forests*.)

SIZE: Small tree (to 30′ tall) or thicket-forming shrub.

LEAVES: Simple, alternate, deciduous. Egg-shaped; 1–4″ long. Margins doubly serrate or lobed and serrate. Commonly have prominent stipules (small, leafy "ears" that grow in pairs where leaves attach to the twig).

FRUIT: Small, black pome (apple) about ¼″ wide.

TWIGS: Short (under 1″ long), stiff thorns. No terminal bud. Reddish brown.

BARK: Thin; shallow fissures to scaly.

Black hawthorn *Crataegus douglasii*

Common native. Black hawthorn, also called Douglas hawthorn or black haw, is common across the Pacific Northwest. It grows as a small tree or in shrubby thickets that provide important cover for birds and small mammals. It grows along streams, fences, ditches, edges of fields and roads, and in forest openings. It likes moist spots and east of the Cascades follows creeks into the dry country, mixing with other small trees. It ranges from southeast Alaska to central Nevada and Montana.

Fruit is the key. Identify black hawthorn by its black fruit and short thorns (often shorter than 1 inch). It has egg-shaped leaves with toothed margins that sometimes start to divide into lobes. It has white blossoms and clusters of black, apple-like fruits about ¼ inch in diameter. Oregon crab apple has somewhat similar leaves but no thorns.

Black hawthorn fruit   Short, woody thorns   White blossoms

Madrones *Arbutus*

The madrone genus contains about 20 species of trees and shrubs worldwide. Three are native to North America, but only one grows in the Pacific Northwest. Although peeling bark is the most distinctive feature of the Northwest's species, not all species of madrone have this characteristic.

Pacific madrone *Arbutus menziesii*

Unique bark. Archibald Menzies, the Scottish physician and naturalist who accompanied explorer George Vancouver to British Columbia in 1792, first described Pacific madrone: "Its peculiar smooth bark of a reddish-brown color will at all times attract the notice of the most superficial observer." Madrone is quickly identified, even from a distance, by its reddish brown, naked-looking upper stems. A thin outer bark is always peeling off those branches, leaving them smooth and greenish. Old bark is brown and doesn't peel, though it can be flaky. Some say madrone sheds its bark instead of its leaves, but the leaves are shed, too, around the middle of their second summer. Pacific madrone is a broadleaved tree, but it's evergreen, with thick, leathery leaves that remain on the tree through the winter and partway into the next growing season. Clusters of orange-red berries (actually drupes) appear in fall, each resembling a tiny orange. Birds feast on them. Earlier in the growing season, honeybees swarm to showy clusters of white to pink urn-shaped flowers.

Peeling bark

Berry-like fruits in fall

Seldom stands straight. Pacific madrone often leans and twists as if seeking a better view of the world; in truth it does not tolerate shade and always seeks the sun. It is popular for gardens and parks despite some bother from its summer-long shedding of leaves and bark.

Attractive wood. Despite an adequate supply of marketable trees and handsome, cherry-colored wood, Pacific madrone sees only limited use because its wood tends to warp and check as it dries. Its heavy, dense wood makes fine fuel.

SIZE: Grows to 100' tall and 6' in diameter. Often has multiple stems arising from buds at the root collar.

LEAVES: Simple, alternate, evergreen. Oblong; 3–5" long; thick and leathery; dark green above and light green below. Edges smooth or finely serrated.

FRUIT: Small (pea size), round, orange-red, berrylike fruit with a pebbly texture.

TWIGS: Stout; smooth; may be green, orange, or reddish-brown.

BARK: Flakes off in scales or strips; outer bark is orange or reddish-brown; inner bark may be bright green.

Pacific madrone is a broadleaved evergreen.

Maples *Acer*

Maples constitute one of the largest, most diverse, and most important groups of broadleaved trees in the world. There are about 125 species of maples, most living in China and eastern Asia. Maples are noted for their leaves, which grow opposite each other and have palmately arranged lobes and veins, and their propellerlike seeds, called samaras.

Bigleaf maples dot the hillsides of the Pacific Northwest with blazing color each fall.

Vine maple, a large shrub and sometimes a small tree, lights up the understory in fall.

PHOTO: U.S. FOREST SERVICE

Thirteen maples are native to North America; three are native to Oregon and Washington: bigleaf, vine, and Rocky Mountain maples. Bigleaf maple is a large tree; vine and Rocky Mountain maples usually grow as large shrubs. A second tree-sized maple, boxelder, is not native here, but has been planted and escaped cultivation to the point where it is quite common.

Large trees

Single stem; broad crown

BIGLEAF MAPLE: Leaves are commonly 6 to 12 inches in diameter (sometimes larger) with prominent lobes and deep sinuses; samaras (helicopterlike fruit) grow at right angles to one another and have fuzzy heads.

BOXELDER: Though it doesn't have "maple" in its name, it's still an *Acer*. Native to much of the U.S., it's an invader in the Pacific Northwest — planted and escaped cultivation. Its leaves are opposite, but pinnately compound (rather than simple) with three to seven leaflets (the only North American maple with compound leaves). Its fruits are double-winged samaras. For more on boxelder, see page 132.

Large shrubs — but occasionally small trees

Multiple stems; usually under 25 feet tall

ROCKY MOUNTAIN MAPLE: Leaves typically are simple and palmately lobed with three main lobes; sometimes compound on the same plant; 2 to 5 inches wide. Fruits are double samaras that grow approximately at right angles to one another; they hang in small clusters.

VINE MAPLE: Leaves are simple and palmately lobed with five to nine lobes; commonly 2 to 4 inches in diameter; form a circular perimeter. Fruits are double samara that grow at 180-degree angles to one another and do not have fuzzy heads.

Bigleaf maple *Acer macrophyllum*

Aptly named. Bigleaf maple gets its name from the size of its leaves. They're palmately lobed and usually 6 to 12 inches wide but can stretch to 15 inches — the largest of the world's many species of maples. The leaf stem is almost as long as the leaf. Its leaf stalk (petiole) is nearly as long as its leaf blade, and the petiole exudes a milky sap when broken. No other Northwestern maple does this, although the common ornamental Norway maple does.

PHOTO: U.S. FOREST SERVICE

Bigleaf maple in fall near Mosier, Oregon.

Bigleaf maple leaves resemble a human hand with the fingers outspread; each leaf has five main lobes. The uppermost lobe has a distinct waist — it appears almost as if someone has pulled a belt around its midsection.

Like a hand, each leaf has five main "fingers."

Fruits are sets of double samaras

Cluster of maple flowers

Typically, two samaras join to form a V, and unlike other Northwestern maples, the seeds of bigleaf are covered with dense hairs.

Where bigleaf maple grows. Bigleaf maple grows on the west side of the Cascades and Sierra Nevada from British Columbia through most of California. It prefers moist, well-drained soils and is one of the most common broadleaved trees in the valleys and foothills of its home range. Its leaves are high in base nutrients and play an important role in enriching the soil when they decompose.

Uses. When grown in the open, bigleaf maple tends to have a stubby trunk and an immense crown. As a result, it's a common native

SIZE: Grows to 100' tall and 4' in diameter.

LEAVES: Simple, opposite, and deciduous. Very large. Palmately lobed (5 lobes) with the central lobe having a distinct "waist." Long leaf stalk exudes milky sap.

FRUIT: Double samaras in long clusters; samaras joined at right angles; hairy seeds.

TWIGS: Buds and branchlets are opposite.

BARK: Grayish or reddish-brown; interlacing ridges and furrows.

shade tree in western Oregon and Washington. It often can be found spreading a carpet of shade over parks and schoolyards and nestling over backyards like a broody hen. Its tendency to produce huge burls at the base of the tree makes bigleaf maple a prized furniture wood. Burls contain contorted grain patterns and "birds' eyes" that result in striking veneers and novelties. Many burls are exported to Italy and France to be worked by skilled craftsmen into fine furniture and musical instruments. In the fall, bigleaf maple's bright yellow foliage splashes color over hills that tend to be dominated by dark green conifers. Bigleaf maples produce huge crops of seeds each year, and you'll often see squirrels, birds, and other small creatures enjoying a picnic beneath their spreading crowns. Bigleaf maple also makes fine firewood.

Rocky Mountain maple *Acer glabrum*

Rocky Mountain maple is common east of the Cascades.

Different leaves. The growth form of Rocky Mountain maple is similar to that of vine maple, but its leaves are quite different. In fact, Rocky Mountain maple has two distinctly different kinds of leaves. Its typical leaves are simple and palmately lobed with three main lobes each with serrated edges; each leaf is 2 to 5 inches across. Infrequently, the leaves may be divided into three separate leaflets, resulting in palmately compound leaves. Sometimes, both kinds of leaves occur on the same plant. Fruits are samaras; each samara is about 1 inch long; they grow in pairs at nearly right angles to each other. The plant usually forms a clump of slender stems with up-pointing branches 10 to 20 feet tall; it tends to be less sprawling than vine maple.

Common east of the Cascade crest. This is the most common maple east of the Cascade crest. Although it grows throughout the state, it's harder to find in the Coast Range and western Cascades. Two good places to see it are along roads in the high country of southern Oregon and in the broken lava fields of central Oregon. This tree seems to like rocky places, canyon walls, and mountain creeks, yet it often hides in the deep woods. Rocky Mountain maple has a wider range than other Oregon maples, ranging as far east as South Dakota and Nebraska and as far south as New Mexico and Arizona.

SIZE: Generally under 20′ tall and several inches in diameter.

LEAVES: Typically simple, opposite, deciduous, with 3 lobes; sometimes palmately compound with 3 leaflets. Margins serrated. Typically 2–5″ in diameter.

FRUIT: Double samaras joined at nearly right angles to one another.

TWIGS: Opposite buds and branchlets. Buds have 2 dark red scales.

BARK: Smooth with a greenish tinge.

Typical leaf, at left, and compound leaf, right.

Douglas maple. A variety of Rocky Mountain maple, Douglas maple (*Acer glabrum* var. *douglasii*), grows sparsely in western Oregon and widely east of the Cascades, stretching north into Alaska. It has shallower leaf indentations than Rocky Mountain maple and nearly parallel seed wings. Leaf shape varies so much within the species that the two varieties are difficult to tell apart. Sometimes the two names are used as synonyms for the same plant.

Cultural uses. Native people of western North America used the branches of vine and Rocky Mountain maple for snowshoes and other goods that needed thin, tough branches that could be bent and intertwined. The inner bark was woven into rope.

Vine maple *Acer circinatum*

Red fall colors of vine maple growing beneath conifers.

Pinwheels and propellers. Vine maple leaves generally have seven lobes that radiate out from the point where the leaf joins its stalk. When the tips of the lobes are connected in "dot-to-dot" fashion, the leaf resembles a child's pinwheel. Its seeds are easy to distinguish from those of bigleaf — in vine maple they resemble an airplane propeller. No other tree or shrub in the Northwest woods can match vine maple's glowing fall colors of yellow, orange and red. They often make the fall woods seem afire.

Where vine maple grows. Look for clumps of stems, usually under 20 feet tall, growing beneath towering conifers like Douglas-fir and western hemlock. Vine maple likes damp places and fairly good soil — prime timber growing sites. It survives heavy shade but also can grow in the full sun. Vine maple grows primarily west of the Cascade crest.

Octopus of the forest. In heavy shade, older vine maples may have long, crooked stems creeping over the ground in search of light. Limbs often root where they touch the ground, sometimes forming an elaborate network of moss-draped arches. To Northwest woodsmen, there is no obstacle course like a vine maple thicket. Pioneer French-Canadian trappers called it "devil wood." Deer and elk have a different opinion — they browse it eagerly — and birds and small mammals love its seeds. When overstory trees are harvested, vine maple can expand rapidly, making reforestation with conifers difficult.

SIZE: Generally, under 20′ tall with multiple stems several inches in diameter.

LEAVES: Simple, opposite, deciduous. Palmately lobed with 5–9 lobes (usually 7). Average 2–4″ in diameter. Circular outline.

FRUIT: Double samaras that resemble an airplane propeller.

TWIGS: Opposite buds and branchlets. Twigs often end in 2 buds (resulting in dichotomous branching).

BARK: Smooth with a greenish tinge.

Vine maple flowers

Leaf and samara

Curlleaf mountain-mahogany

Mountain-mahoganies *Cercocarpus*

A tiny, hard seed topped by a feathery tail is a characteristic that clearly separates mountain-mahoganies from other trees and shrubs. Some mountain-mahoganies are deciduous, others are evergreen, and some seem to straddle the line. There are about 10 species of mountain-mahogany, all of which grow only in the western United States. The hyphen in the common name alerts us that this group of small trees and shrubs is not related to the true mahoganies that grow in the tropics. It's not uncommon to call a member of this genus by its scientific name, *Cercocarpus*.

Two species are native to the Northwest. Both grow primarily as shrubs, but both also sometimes grow as small trees, often with multiple trunks.

- **Birchleaf mountain-mahogany:** Small leaves are egg-shaped; edges are serrated toward the tip but smooth near the base. Evergreen, but sometimes just barely (old leaves may fall off as new leaves emerge).

- **Curlleaf mountain-mahogany:** Small leaves are narrow, tough, and leathery; edges are smooth and curled under. Evergreen.

Birchleaf mountain-mahogany

Cercocarpus betuloides

Resembles curlleaf. Birchleaf mountain-mahogany is similar to curlleaf mountain-mahogany in size and habit but differs in that it has a toothed leaf resembling a small alder or birch leaf. The thick, smooth leaves are more or less evergreen (old leaves may fall off as new leaves emerge in spring or may last a second growing season). On young twigs, leaves arise singly; on older twigs, leaves most often are clustered on spur shoots. The white plumed tail on the seed is 2 to 3 inches long.

SIZE: An erect shrub to 15′ tall or a small tree to 40′ tall.

LEAVES: Simple, alternate (and clustered on spur shoots), evergreen (often just barely). Obovate in shape; ½–2″ wide; serrated above the midpoint and entire below.

FRUIT: A single seed topped by a white, feathery tail up to 3″ long.

TWIGS: Slender; reddish brown; spur shoots. Gray to reddish brown.

BARK: Thin and smooth on young trees, becoming scaly with age.

Likes the coast. Along the Pacific Coast, birchleaf mountain-mahogany likes the dry foothills and lower mountain slopes of the Coast Ranges and the Sierra Nevada. It also grows in the southern Oregon Cascades and southeastward into Arizona. It does not grow in Washington.

Uses. Birchleaf mountain-mahogany is browsed by deer and is used by humans for fuel and for turnery items such as bowls and novelties.

Birchleaf mountain-mahogany: leaves serrated at their apex; seeds with long, plumed tails

Curlleaf mountain-mahogany

Cercocarpus ledifolius

Known by its silver streamer. Curlleaf mountain-mahogany has a silky streamer 1 to 3 inches long attached to each seed, so recognition is easy when fruit is present. Tiny evergreen leaves with margins curled under make identification easy year-round (besides giving curlleaf its name). Curlleaf mountain-mahogany usually is twisted and unshapely because of its struggle with the forces of nature, including browsing animals and a severe climate. Twigs are stiff and almost thornlike. Leaves have a resinous odor.

The silky streamers and curled, leathery leaves of curlleaf mountain-mahogany

SIZE: An erect shrub to 15′ tall or a small tree to 40′ tall and 2′ in diameter.

LEAVES: Simple, alternate (and clustered on spur shoots), evergreen. Elliptical; ½–1″ long; thick and leathery; edges curled under.

FRUIT: A single seed ½″ long with a feathery tail up to 3″ long.

TWIGS: Spur shoots common.

BARK: Furrows and ridges that break into platelike scales. Red- or gray-brown.

Where to find it. Look for these tough, shrubby trees growing in scattered groups and tangled thickets across eastern Oregon; they just barely touch southeastern Washington. They typically grow on dry, rocky ridges, in the understory of open pine forests, or scattered across sagebrush flats. Truly a tree of the Southwest, curlleaf ranges from southern Oregon to southern California and east through most of the Rockies.

Uses. The wood of this species has a beautiful mahogany color, taking a high polish and resulting in its common name. It's very hard and so heavy it will not float. It's a long-burning fuel that gives off intense heat and commonly is used to smoke meats. In some areas, it's an important browse species for deer and elk. Mountain-mahogany often grows in short, dense, tangled stands where many animals find protection both from the weather and from hunters.

Oaks *Quercus*

As the lion symbolizes courage, so the oak stands for strength, inspiring the Roman poet Virgil to write nearly 2,000 years ago: "Full in the midst of his own strength he stands, stretching his brawny arms and leafy hands."

Oaks are one of the largest and most diverse groups of trees in the world — about 500 species worldwide and 60 in North America. Oaks come in all shapes and sizes. Some have huge, wide-spreading crowns, others are small shrubs; some are evergreen, others are deciduous; some grow on very wet sites, others tolerate extreme drought; some have lobed leaves, others are unlobed. Four features that all oaks share are acorns, flowers borne in short catkins, star-shaped piths (the inner core of the twig), and clusters of large buds at the tips of their twigs.

Fortunately for those of us trying to identify them, only three oaks native to Oregon and Washington reach tree size, but many more are planted in lawns and parks throughout the state. Three additional natives grow only as shrubs, but they are typically considered varieties of the other species and will not be described here.

- **California black oak:** Leaves have pointed lobes with bristle tips; acorns have deep caps.

- **Canyon live oak:** Small evergreen leaves may have either smooth or spiked edges (on the same branch); acorns have variable sized caps.

- **Oregon white oak:** Leaves have rounded lobes; acorns have shallow caps.

Open-grown Oregon white oaks are noted for wide-spreading, gnarly limbs. If unburned, oak habitats can be overrun by conifers and other hardwoods.

One characteristic common to all oaks: a star-shaped pith, or center, of twigs.

It's worth noting that California is a hotbed for oaks — 19 species in all plus many hybrids; Nine grow as trees while 10 grow as shrubs. They come in many shapes and sizes; some are deciduous but many are evergreen, with small, tough, waxy leaves adapted to drought; some prefer moist valley sites while others prefer hot, dry hillsides; and others prefer the misty coast. Many grow only in California while others grow throughout the Southwest. California oaks that do not extend into the Pacific Northwest will not be described here. All of the oaks described below are also native to California.

California black oak *Quercus kelloggii*

Pointed lobes. Sharply pointed and bristle-tipped leaves of California black oak distinguish it from other West Coast oaks. However, many nonnative oaks that resemble California black oak have been planted in towns throughout the Pacific Northwest. In addition to pointed leaves, look for acorn caps that cover over half the nut (the caps of most other oaks are shallower). Viewed at a

The acorns of California black oak have deep caps.

distance, California black oaks often resemble maples because of their rounded crowns and shiny, dark green leaves. This tree seldom grows straight but leans like a sailor who has not found his "land legs." The common name refers to the very dark bark of older trees.

The pointed lobes of California black oak leaves

Range. As its name implies, California black oak is most common in California, but it grows as far north as the Umpqua Valley in Oregon. Douglas, Josephine, and Jackson counties contain nearly all the black oaks in Oregon. California black oaks like sun and thrive where it's hot and dry, especially on lower hills and on broad valley bottoms.

Food locker. Acorn woodpeckers do a curious thing to this tree (and to other oaks that develop thick, furrowed bark). They drill holes in the bark just the right size to hold acorns and then hammer them in. That way squirrels can't get them. Many such "food lockers" are seen in oak trees of southwestern Oregon — not to mention in telephone poles, barns and house siding! Acorns are also a favorite food of other birds and mammals and were eaten by humans in earlier days, after being soaked in water to remove most of the acidic tannin.

Uses. Today, black oak is used primarily for firewood. But it has possibilities for flooring, furniture, hardware and other products. Black oak is shorter lived than Oregon white oak — it tends to develop rot with age.

SIZE: Grows to 80′ tall and 3′ in diameter, but usually is smaller.

LEAVES: Simple, alternate, deciduous. Pinnately lobed with 7 pointed and bristle-tipped lobes.

FRUIT: Acorn with deep cap; 1–2″ long.

TWIGS: Stout, with buds clustered near the tip.

BARK: Dark with irregular plates; about 1″ thick.

Male catkins shed pollen in spring

Canyon live oak *Quercus chrysolepis*

Some leaves of canyon live oak resemble holly; others have smooth edges.

Split personality. Canyon live oak has a split personality. Two kinds of leaves grow on the same tree; one looks like holly with sharp-pointed spines along their margins, the other has smooth edges. The younger the tree, the more holly-like leaves it has.

What's in a name? This tree's name tells us something important about it. Live oak refers to the fact that it's evergreen, rather than deciduous; that is, its leaves live several years before falling off, so the tree is always covered with leaves. Canyon refers to the fact that it likes to grow on canyon sides and bottoms, especially those that are hot and dry.

Range. Where it has favorable soil and moisture, canyon live oak can reach 80 feet or more. Like most other trees, it assumes a shape according to the space in which it has to grow. The live oaks of the southeastern United States are celebrated for their wide, spreading crowns. When growing in the open on good ground, canyon live oak may also do this. However, most grow in rough, dry country where they compete for light and assume any shape needed to acquire light; some grow as small trees or bushes.

SIZE: May be a shrub to 15' tall or a tree to 80' tall and 2' in diameter.

LEAVES: Two distinctive types on same plant. All are simple, alternate, evergreen; 1–4" long. Some have smooth edges, while some are spiked like holly leaves.

FRUIT: Acorn from ½–2" long. Cap varies in depth.

TWIGS: Slender; buds clustered at tips. Pith is star-shape.

BARK: Grayish brown and scaly. Thin (about 1" thick).

Canyon live oak is an evergreen broadleaf.

Tough wood. One of the local names for this tree is "maul oak" because farmers and loggers once sought the extremely heavy, tough wood to make mauls for driving stakes, pegs and nails. The wood also was used for wagon axles and wheels. Canyon live oak is not commercially valuable at present. Dense, shining foliage and attractive form recommend it as an ornamental, especially in dry regions of the state.

Canyon live oak acorns

Oregon white oak *Quercus garryana*

Valley tree. In 1826, explorer David Douglas noted that the low hills of western Oregon were covered with oaks. Today Oregon white oak still grows in the interior valleys of western Oregon and Washington, but the forests have a different look. The open oak-grass savanna that Douglas saw was a product of frequent fires set by lightning and by Northwest Indians to improve food for deer and elk. Because of fire suppression the

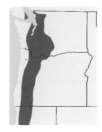

Oregon white oak leaves have rounded lobes.

Wasp galls, left. At right, an Oregon white oak acorn featuring a shallow cap.

past 100 years, conifers have taken over many of the open oak forests. Despite this, Oregon white oak is still a prominent feature of the interior valleys. Oregon white oak grows throughout the Siskiyou Mountains but seldom west of the Coast Range summit. Only along the Columbia Gorge does it venture east of the Cascade crest.

Rounded lobes. Oregon white oak is the only oak native to Oregon and Washington with rounded lobes on its leaves, although several introduced species also have this characteristic. Its acorns have a shallow cap, almost like a beret sitting atop a head.

Distinctive form. Before middle age, open-grown trees have a "trimmed" look. A short, stubby trunk will proliferate into a thicket of twisting limbs, sometimes suggesting writhing snakes. In old age, 200 to 500 years, the short, massive trunk and heavy, gnarled limbs are unmistakable. These craggy survivors are scattered in such havens as suburbs, farmsteads, parks, college campuses and public grounds. They draw our attention, for they are lords of the land — offering us endless visual pleasure. Landscapers like this oak because of its interesting form, tolerance of town conditions, longevity and deep rooting, which permits garden plants to grow beneath scattered shade trees. Oregon white oaks are intolerant of shade and do not like heavy watering in the summer. As a result of their dislike of shade, when growing in clusters, the entire group assumes the shape of a ball, with most of the leaves along the outer surface.

Little used commercially. Oregon white oak has good-quality wood suitable for flooring, furniture, ship-building, crossties and many other

SIZE: Grows to 80' tall and 3' in diameter. Has a rounded crown when grown in the open.

LEAVES: Simple, alternate, deciduous. Pinnately lobed with 7–9 rounded lobes; lobes often irregular. 3–6" long and 2–5" wide.

FRUIT: Acorn with shallow cap; about 1" long.

TWIGS: Stout; several buds clustered at tip; fuzzy buds. Pith is star-shaped.

BARK: Grayish; may be shaggy or have shallow ridges and fissures.

Craggy oak bark

uses. It has been little used, however, probably because eastern forests provide ample supplies of oak, and our oaks tend to be scattered and short-trunked. A white oak heartwood post near Eugene lasted for 100 years, showing how durable the heartwood is, even without preservatives.

More about white oak. White oak leaves have a protein content nearly equal to alfalfa hay and are browsed by livestock, deer and other animals. After a disastrous snowfall in 1880, Willamette Valley settlers saved many of their cattle by feeding them white oak twigs and bark. Garry oak is another common name for this tree. Because Nicholas Garry, secretary of the Hudson's Bay Company, helped botanist David Douglas, he is remembered in the scientific name of this species.

Poppers. Each summer and fall, children delight in stomping the leaves of Oregon white oak — not because they're angry, but to pop the round galls that live on the underside of many leaves. These galls are actually the homes of gall wasps. Don't worry — these wasps do not harm people. They lay their eggs inside oak leaves, and the leaves react by creating a hard, brittle covering that protects the wasps in their larval stage. In mid to late summer, a heavily infested oak grove may rattle with the sound of the larvae trying to break out of this protective covering.

Tanoaks *Notholithocarpus* • Formerly *Lithocarpus*

Until recently tanoaks were classified in the genus *Lithocarpus,* which included one or two species in North America and nearly 100 species in southeastern Asia. But currently, taxonomists are reconsidering how to classify this genus, with most opting for a new genus specifically for the tanoaks of North America.

Tanoaks are related to oaks and chestnuts.

SIZE: Grows to 100' tall and 3' in diameter, but also may be shrubby.

LEAVES: Simple, alternate, evergreen. Thick and leathery; 3–5" long; bluish-white fuzz underneath; margins smooth or toothed, often on the same twig.

FRUIT: Acorns with soft-spiked caps.

TWIGS: Stout; buds clustered at tips; star-shaped pith.

BARK: Thin with flattened ridges or plates.

Regardless of which scientific name we choose, all tanoaks are an evolutionary link between the oaks and the chestnuts, with nuts similar to those of acorns, but enclosed in a bristly burr, reminiscent of chestnuts. The only tanoak native to North America grows in California and Oregon. Because tanoak is not a true oak, its name is written as one word rather than two; it can also be hyphenated, but that is less common.

Tanoak *Notholithocarpus densiflorus*
Formerly *Lithocarpus densiflorus*

Unique hat. Tanoak's acorn cap is a sure way to identify the species. Bristles stick out around the cap, like the crown on the Statue of Liberty, but they are soft rather than spiny. A single evergreen leaf also will identify tanoak. Mature leaves are thick and leathery and often have a bluish white fuzz on the underside. Veins on the surface are uniformly spaced and create a washboard look. Edges of the leaves can be smooth or have widely spaced teeth.

Variable growth form. Tanoak can be tall and narrow in closed stands, or short-trunked and spreading in the open. Shrubby forms climb high into the Siskiyou Mountains of Oregon, while those growing in the coastal fog belt readily attain 100-foot heights. If the main stem is cut or burned, buds at the base of the trunk and stored in underground burls rapidly sprout, resulting in clumps of multiple stems.

Abundant hardwood. Tanoak is one of the four most abundant hardwoods in Oregon; 85 percent of its timber volume lies in Curry County in southwestern Oregon. It grows only in southwestern Oregon and California, from sea level to about 5,000 feet; at higher elevations it is often shrubby.

Tanoak often sprouts multiple stems, top. Thick, leathery leaves are fuzzy underneath, row two. Male flowers in long, fuzzy spikes, above left, and acorns with bristly caps, above right.

Sudden Oak Death. Even though it's not a true oak, tanoak is affected by a serious plant disease called Sudden Oak Death (*Phytophthora ramorum*). First discovered in California in the early 1990s, this disease already has killed tens of thousands of trees from central California to southern Oregon. Many species of trees and shrubs are hosts and carriers: coast live oak, California black oak, Douglas-fir, grand fir, coast redwood, Pacific rhododendron, and at least one species of wildflower. Good sanitation is a vital part of limiting the spread of this disease. If you work in or travel through forests dominated by tanoak, be sure to check with the nearest office of the Oregon Department of Forestry, USDA Forest Service or Oregon State University Extension Service for appropriate sanitation for your clothing, tools and vehicle when you leave the woods.

Uses. Tanoak is fine for plywood, flooring, furniture and papermaking, but industrial use is limited. The bark once was important in tanning leather — hence the name tanoak, or tanbark oak. Many Northwest Indian communities once relied heavily on tanoak acorns, which they ground, leached and cooked in many ways.

Walnuts *Juglans*

Worldwide, there are about 21 species of *Juglans*, spanning temperate regions across Europe and Asia, as well as North and South America. Six species of walnuts grow in North America, both as large trees and shrubs. Two species are native to the West Coast, California walnut and Hinds walnut, although only Hinds walnut crosses the northern California border into Oregon. Walnuts are deciduous trees noted for large, pinnately compound leaves, a chambered pith and large woody shelled seeds borne inside a leathery outer covering. Their seeds are important sources of food for humans and wildlife alike, and are commonly grown both as ornamentals and as food crops.

Hinds walnut *Juglans hindsii*

Rare in Oregon.
Hinds walnut grows almost exclusively in California, primarily surrounding San Francisco Bay; even within this range it is quite rare. Many sources do not consider it part of the Northwest flora, but there is a small, scattered set of individuals in the Rogue Valley of southwestern Oregon. Despite its rarity, some stumps

Hinds walnut has large, pinnately compound leaves and yellow-green outer husks that turn black with age.

in Oregon have been aged at over 300 years. Like California buckeye and other chaparral associates, it may have marched northward from California several thousand years ago, near the end of the last glacial period. Some consider Hinds a variety of California walnut; hence part of the controversy over its existence in Oregon. Throughout its range Hinds walnut is primarily a riparian species, growing on the silty deposits from streams and rivers.

How to identify it. This is a medium-to-large tree, commonly growing 30 to 60 feet tall, with trunk diameters up to 5 to 6 feet. The pinnately compound leaves are about 1 foot long with 13 to 21 lance-shaped leaflets with toothed margins; each leaflet is 2 to 5 inches long. The nut has a smooth, thick, brown shell, with a small edible meat inside; each nut is borne singly, inside a leathery, indehiscent (non-splitting) leathery cover. This heavy nut is distributed primarily by water; hence its distribution along rivers and floodplains.

SIZE: Grows 30–60' tall and several feet in diameter; commonly with a single trunk.

LEAVES: Pinnately compound, about 1 foot long, with 13–21 toothed leaflets alternately arranged; deciduous. Lance-shaped leaflets commonly 2–5" long. Vein angles have tufts of hair.

FRUIT: Thick, hard shelled nut borne inside an indehiscent outer husk; about 1" in diameter. Small, edible meat inside.

TWIGS: Thick with chambered pith; alternately arranged.

BARK: Dark gray-black with irregular ridges and furrows.

The shells of Hinds walnut are nearly smooth.

Uses. Hinds walnut is commonly used as a rootstock for English (and other) walnuts, and the richly grained wood is typically marketed to woodworkers as clarno walnut. Northwest Indians added walnuts to jerky and dried fruits to form a high energy food called pemmican. Though not common in Oregon, in 1947 a Hinds walnut tree there measured 9 feet in diameter and 80 feet tall — the world's largest recorded specimen.

Its future in Oregon. Its rarity and scattered distribution put it at risk from logging, land development, agriculture, sand and gravel mining, and the planting of non-native walnuts which may hybridize with it. Special care is needed to ensure its future in Oregon.

Willows *Salix*

As a group, willows are easy to identify, but distinguishing different types of willows is hard because there are so many — North America has about 90 different types — and many species interbreed and produce offspring with characteristics of both parents.

Pacific willow leaf and rounded stipules.

Form and location are important. All North American willows grow as shrubs, but perhaps a dozen also grow to tree size. Regardless of size, they typically have multiple stems and indistinct crowns. Willows grow almost anywhere but most often along streams and on wet ground. Some even grow near treeline as prostrate shrubs.

Leaves. Although not all willow leaves are identical, they have a particular look about them — almost like children in the same family. They tend to be narrow and pointed, and are generally yellow-green on top and white below. As a result, wind moving through the willows makes them flutter. They all have short petioles (leaf stalks) and most have leafy "ears" (stipules) where each leaf joins its twig.

Flowers and fruit. Who has not collected "pussywillows," the earliest harbingers of spring? These are actually the male, pollen-bearing flower of willows. Male and female flowers are on separate plants (dioecious), so some flowers turn into tear-shape fruits filled with cottony seeds, and others simply wilt and fall off. The cottony seeds are distributed both by wind and water. Regardless of how they are distributed, they are very tiny and need to land on moist soil soon after being dropped or they will dry out and die.

Buds and twigs. Willows are readily distinguished from other trees by narrow winter buds that hug the twig. Each bud is covered by a single caplike scale that resembles a stocking cap pulled down over it. There is never a terminal bud on willows; the twigs simply die back to a lateral bud in winter. Willow twigs are often yellowish-green, sometimes with tinges of purple or red. Have you ever noticed a vivid yellow or red haze hanging over creeks or gullies in late winter? It's likely to be the colorful stems of willows reminding us that spring is near. These showy willow thickets are especially common east of the Cascades.

Uses. Willows of our region typically don't reach commercial size, yet they perform great service in reducing stream bank erosion because of their clinging roots and tangled branches. Baskets made of long, supple willow twigs were among the earliest manufactured products of humans. Now, willow twigs are used to make lawn furniture, and the tough, springy wood is used to make croquet balls and cricket bats. Introduced species such as weeping willow and golden willow are common shade and ornamental trees. Many species of wildlife like to eat willow twigs and flowers. Rabbits, mice, beaver, grouse and other wildlife eat willow bark; deer, moose and livestock browse the stems. While we may not always notice the willows, other eyes do not overlook them.

Willows are nearly everywhere. If you are camping, look for willows along lakes and streams. If dry, it's a superior wood for fires and camp stoves. Willow is short lived, so dead trees or limbs are always available. Willows may be small and humble, but they grow abundantly where animals gather, as all must have water. Willows stand water as well as any tree known and even grow well on poorly drained land. They sprout easily from stumps and even from pieces of branch or root that break off from the parent plant and are buried in soil.

Some Pacific Northwest tree-size willows

- **HOOKER WILLOW** (*Salix hookeriana*): A beach willow found the full length of the Northwest coast and seldom more than 5 miles from salt water. Its location and wide leaf improve chances of identification. It can be found along streams and on swampy ground, near sea level.

- **NORTHWEST WILLOW** (*Salix sessilifolia*): Has long, narrow leaves, often 10 times as long as they are wide. It grows in the western Cascades of Oregon, is uncommon in Washington, and reappears in southwestern British Columbia. It's also called sandbar willow.

- **PACIFIC WILLOW** (*Salix lasiandra*): A black-barked tree or large shrub found around wet places. It often reaches 40 to 60 feet tall and is abundant west of the Cascades at low and moderate elevations. Identification is aided by two or more tiny nodules at the base of each leaf blade. It's also called black willow.

- **PEACHLEAF WILLOW** (*Salix amygdaloides*): Found along streams and around farm homes in extreme northeastern Oregon and southeastern Washington. This is the largest willow east of the Cascades, sometimes 70 feet tall.

- **SCOULER WILLOW** (*Salix scouleriana*): Probably the most common willow in western North America. It grows not only at low elevations but on higher mountains. In western Oregon and Washington, it often reaches 40 feet tall. Unlike other willows, it thrives away from water. It's also called mountain willow.

- **SITKA WILLOW** (*Salix sitchensis*): Grows along the Pacific coast from San Francisco into Alaska, with scattered appearances in eastern Oregon and Washington. Leaves are typically oval to lanceolate but some have a pear-shaped outline. It's also called silky willow because of satiny hairs on the undersides of its leaves.

Cottony seeds

Rounded stipules

Male pollen-bearing flowers

Typical willow leaf with bud pressed closely against twig

Non-native species enrich Northwest landscapes

Though most of the trees inhabiting our forests are native to the Pacific Northwest, most of the shade, fruit and ornamental trees that grace our lives are not. Hundreds of species of trees have been introduced from elsewhere in the United States and the world. Because these are the trees that dominate our yards, streets and public grounds, they're often interwoven more closely with our daily lives than are our native trees.

This section describes some, but by no means all, of the Northwest's most common and important introduced trees. Because our climate permits all but the most tropical of trees to thrive here, a complete list would be long, indeed! Therefore, we've selected trees that you're most likely to see, but we do not mean to imply that these are more important than others you might find.

Trees within this section are listed alphabetically by the common name of their genus. Most can be identified by using the keys that appear earlier in this book.

An elegant line of elms in Corvallis, Oregon. The broad, spreading crowns cast dense shade, but elms are susceptible to Dutch elm disease.

PHOTO: KARL MAASDAM
© OREGON STATE
UNIVERSITY

Common introduced conifers

Arborvitae *Thuja* spp. • several species

Many of the Northwest's most beautiful hedges are formed from these adaptable evergreen conifers. There are about five species of *Arborvitae* in the world, all related to our native western redcedar. They all have scalelike leaves arranged in flattened sprays and small, upturned cones that often resemble woody rosebuds. Many varieties grow tall and slender and can be pruned into a variety of forms — good attributes for hedges. Several other genera contain members that are sometimes, although incorrectly, called arborvitae, including *Chamaecyparis* (false cypress), *Thujopsis* (hiba arborvitae), and *Platycladus* (oriental arborvitae); they each have characteristics similar to *Thuja*, but also their own distinguishing features.

Arborvitae hedge

Cedars or 'true' cedars *Cedrus* spp. • many species

True cedars are native to the Middle East and Himalayan regions of the world and are very different from the scale-leaved false cedars native to the Pacific Northwest. True cedars have evergreen needles borne in dense clusters on stout, woody pegs (similar to larches, only evergreen). Their large, barrel-shaped cones stick up above their branches and have thin scales that fall apart when mature (similar to true firs). Three true cedars commonly are planted in the Northwest:

Deodar cedar (*Cedrus deodara*): The largest, most common, and easiest to recognize of the true cedars. It commonly surpasses 125 feet in height and several feet in diameter. Its needles are 1 to 2 inches long and are yellow-green to blue-green. Needles are borne both singly on young shoots and in dense clusters of 20 to 30 on spur shoots on older branches. Branch tips and the leader droop noticeably, similar to western hemlock. Cones are large (3 to 5 inches long), borne upright on their branches, and fall apart scale-by-scale, similar to true firs. Deodar cedar is native to the Himalayan Mountains of India and Pakistan, where it is a commercially important tree. It is used in construction of temples and houseboats, in making incense, and for its essential oils. It is the national tree of Pakistan.

Atlas or Atlantic cedar (*Cedrus atlantica*): Similar to Deodar cedar except that it is a smaller tree (up to 100 feet tall), has shorter needles (about 1 inch long) and slightly smaller cones (2 to 3 inches long). In addition, its needles have a blue-green color and a distinctive white bloom. Atlas cedar is named for its

Deodar cedar

homeland in the Atlas Mountains of northwestern Africa where it is threatened by overuse from timber harvest, grazing, and the like. As a result, there are large reforestation efforts in some regions. One ornamental variety of this species assumes a dramatic weeping appearance and is commonly used in landscaping as an accent tree.

Cedar of Lebanon (*Cedrus libani*): Nearly identical to Atlas cedar. Both exhibit a stiff branching habit and have blue-green needles about 1 inch long. Cedar of Lebanon has slightly larger cones (3 to 4 inches long). This tree is native to the eastern Mediterranean region where its wood is prized for having a fine grain and a pleasant aroma. Reportedly, this was the primary tree used to build King Solomon's temple. Heavy harvesting through the centuries has limited its range and abundance, but current reforestation efforts are trying to reverse that trend. It is the national tree of Lebanon.

Cedar of Lebanon

Chinese-fir *Cunninghamia lanceolata*

Chinese-fir is native to China and parts of Southeast Asia. The hyphen reminds us that it is not really a fir — rather, it is a member of the Cypress family. Its evergreen needles are long (1 to 3 inches) and wide at the base but tapering to a distinct, very sharp point; they have two bands of stomatal bloom on their lower surface. Their cones are very decorative — round, 1 to 2 inches in diameter, and often with a vegetative shoot growing out the end; rather than being tightly closed, their scales flare at their ends. They often show up in cone wreaths sold in craft stores. The wood of Chinese-fir has properties similar to western redcedar and is often imported into the U.S. as "Chinese cedar," although it is not truly a cedar.

Chinese-fir

Cypress *Cupressus* spp. *or Hesperocyparis* spp. • many species

Cypresses are attractive evergreen conifers that come in a variety of shapes, sizes and colors. Their scalelike foliage resembles that of the junipers, except that cypresses do not typically have sharp-pointed needles mixed in with their scalelike needles. Their round, woody cones resemble those of Port-Orford- and Alaska-cedars, although cypress cones are much larger (often ½ to 2 inches in diameter); juniper cones resemble berries. Most cypresses (but not all) are drought tolerant and cold hardy.

Monterey cypress (*Cupressus macrocarpa* or *Hesperocyparis macrocarpa*): Merits special attention. While native only to the Monterey Peninsula of California, it is widely planted in cities and towns

Typical cypress form

along the coasts of Oregon and California. It grows to 125 feet but is often flat-topped and uniquely shaped by strong coastal winds; it commonly grows several feet in diameter, but sometimes much larger. Foliage is similar to other cypresses, although it is green, lacking both bloom and resin blisters; cones are similar to other cypresses, but generally larger (1 to 2 inches in diameter). Although large trees may appear to be ancient, they seldom surpass 250 years.

Monterey cypress

Dawn redwood *Metasequoia glyptostroboides*

Based on fossil records, dawn redwoods were once one of the most widespread trees in the northern hemisphere — a genus with over 20 species. For many years they were thought to be extinct, until

Cone

Needles

a small stand was rediscovered in China in 1944. But World War II slowed the news of this discovery. Following the War, in 1948 an expedition from Arnold Arboretum collected seeds and began distributing them to universities around the world. Two of the first dawn redwoods introduced into the United States currently grow in front of Peavy Lodge in the Oregon State University College of Forestry's Peavy Arboretum, 7 miles north of Corvallis. They are among the tallest in the world because of the splendid growing conditions.

Dawn redwood

Although dawn redwood leaves resemble those of the coast redwood (*Sequoia sempervirens*) of northern California, dawn redwood leaves are deciduous, falling from the tree while still attached to their twigs. Their delicate cones, which resemble those of redwood, are often dipped in gold or silver and made into pendants. They are now commonly planted as street trees, but natively, there remain only a few small groves in China.

Giant sequoia or Sierra redwood *Sequoiadendron giganteum*

Giant sequoias are the largest trees ever recorded on Earth and are among the oldest. Heights of 300 feet and diameters of 30 feet are not uncommon; ages often range from 2,000 to 3,000 years, with the oldest being approximately 3,500 years — only bristlecone pines are older. Once widespread, giant sequoias now grow only in the Sierra Nevada Mountains of central California. In olden times, it took days for a team of men to fell one tree, and then dances were held on the stump; a roof over a stump made a home for many settlers; and an entire cavalry unit once spent several winter nights inside a burned-out

Needles

Cone

log — with their horses! Giant sequoias were heavily harvested to help build homes, stores and wooden flumes needed to support the California gold rush of 1849, both locally and in major cities such as San Francisco. Since 1890, all of the large, old giant sequoias have been protected in Yosemite, Kings Canyon, and Sequoia national parks, as well as in smaller individual groves. To this day, none of these ancient

Giant sequoia

trees has been harvested, but they are still lost to fires, disease and windthrow. There have been several attempts at growing giant sequoias in managed plantations, without very much success; due, in part, to their irregular, fluted trunks and dense, persistent branches.

Giant sequoia leaves are short, thick, and sharp-pointed, unlike the leaves of any other American tree. Cones are about the size of a hen's egg (2 to 3 inches long) and nearly as hard as a rock. Bark is reddish brown, stringy and very thick — good protection from insects, disease and fire. When young, giant sequoias have a nearly perfect conical shape, and are often cultivated for Christmas trees.

Giant sequoias are commonly planted as street and ornamental trees, often by those who don't understand how fast and how large they will grow. In only 40 years, some have been known to reach 5 to 6 feet in diameter, and roots can easily push up sidewalks, driveways and foundations. So, don't plant them unless you have a lot of space for them to grow.

Monkey puzzle *Araucaria araucana*

Needles

Female cone

This South American relative of the more famous Norfolk Island pine is native to Argentina and Chile but grows well in the maritime climates of the Pacific Northwest, where it is relatively free of disease and is tolerant of all but the wettest and driest soils. It has interesting triangular leaves that may live up to 24 years, cloaking most of the branches they grow on. Lateral branches are long, and swooping, resembling a monkey's tail.

Male "flowers" are large and pendent; they resemble cones but remain soft. Female cones are large, nearly round, borne upright, and disintegrate at maturity. Male and female "flowers" are usually borne on separate trees, so only some trees bear woody cones.

Pollen cones of monkey puzzle

The odd common name was given to this tree by an Englishman who thought the tree must surely be difficult for monkeys to climb (even though monkeys are not native to the parts of South America where monkey puzzle trees grow). Its long, straight trunks were once prized for lumber, but current use is primarily ornamental. It is the national tree of Chile and is considered endangered.

Pines *Pinus* • many species

With about 110 to 120 species, pines are the largest group of conifers in the world. Many are capable of thriving in the Pacific Northwest. Only three of the most commonly planted are described here.

Austrian or European black pine *(Pinus nigra)*:
Native to the Mediterranean region of the world, this is a large pine generally under 100 feet tall with a crown spread of 20 to 40 feet. It was introduced into the U.S. in 1759, and then carried westward by European immigrants because of its hardiness. During the Dust Bowl, it was commonly planted in shelterbelts to block strong winds and help reduce erosion. This is a two-needled pine with very sharp needles 4 to 6 inches long. Cones are oval, about 1 to 3 inches long.

Austrian or European black pine

Mugo pine *(Pinus mugo)*: Native to high elevations in Europe, mugo pine is most commonly a short, multi-stemmed shrubby tree from several to 20 feet tall. Its needles are borne in 2's and are usually 1 to 3 inches long; cones are typically ¾ to 2 inches long. Although easy enough to contain as an ornamental, when it is planted near more natural environments, it can escape and become invasive.

Mugo pine

Scots or Scotch pine *(Pinus sylvestris)*: Native to cold climates of Europe and Asia. Most easily identified by its short (1 to 2 inches) blue-green needles borne in 2's, and orange-red scaly bark, especially on upper trunks and branches. In Europe it is an important forest tree, planted and harvested for lumber, but in North America it is an ornamental tree and is often planted for Christmas trees.

Spruces *Picea* • several species

There are about 35 species of spruce in the world, growing mostly in cool and cold climates of the northern hemisphere. Many of these are planted as ornamentals in the Northwest; some have interesting dwarf, weeping or very narrow growth forms. Only two will be described here.

Scots or Scotch pine

Colorado blue spruce (Picea pungens): Although many spruces are planted as ornamentals throughout North America, Colorado blue spruce is one of the most common because of its striking blue foliage. A native of the central and southern Rockies, this tree resembles our native Engelmann spruce except for its bluer foliage

Blue needles

and slightly longer cones (up to 4 inches long); each cone scale has a jagged edge. The needles of Colorado blue spruce are about 1 inch long, are four-sided, and are stiff and sharp; most have a distinct blue color, although some are green. As with all spruces, each needle is borne on its own raised woody peg. Although lovely, blue spruce is subject to a number of insects and diseases which cause problems when under cultivation. It is the state tree of Colorado.

Colorado blue spruce

White spruce (Picea glauca): White spruce is common and widely distributed across Canada, the northern Lake States, and northern New England. Opinions currently differ about whether it grows natively in northern Washington. Regardless, it is widely planted as an ornamental. It resembles Engelmann spruce in most

Cone

characteristics. Its needles are short (½ to 1 inch long), blue-green with a whitish bloom, and 4-angled with a sharp tip. Its cones are cylindrical, 1 to 2½ inches long, with rounded (not jagged) edges. It is an important commercial species for lumber and paper-making. It is the state tree of South Dakota.

White spruce

Sugi or Japanese-cedar

Cryptomeria japonica

As the hyphen in the common name indicates, this is not a true cedar. Instead, it is the only species in

Needles

its genus, *Cryptomeria,* and is included in the cypress family. It is native only to Japan, where it is an important forest tree; but it is planted as an ornamental across the temperate regions of the world. It can become a large evergreen

conifer (sometimes reaching over 200 feet tall) with interesting, round cones, ½ to ¾ inch diameter. Its

Sugi or Japanese-cedar

needles are short (¼ to ⅜ inch long) and spirally arranged, superficially similar to those of giant sequoia or Norfolk Island pine. Its foliage often turns purple-to-brown in the fall, looking as if the tree has died, but it returns to green in the spring.

Yew: English yew *Taxus baccata*

Fruits

Its dark green foliage, tolerance to shade, and bright red fruit make English yew a commonly used conifer for hedges and ornamentals. Its ability to be tightly pruned makes it a favorite for topiary.
English yew greatly resembles its cousin, Pacific yew, except that English yew has a much more vigorous, healthy growth form. Fruits and leaves are HIGHLY TOXIC TO HUMANS but can be eaten by birds without harm. Like Pacific yew, English yew produces taxol, which is being used in the fight against some types of cancer. Its strong, springy wood furnished bows for numerous armies of Europe.

English yew

Common introduced broadleaved trees

Apple and crab apple

Malus spp. (formerly included in the *Pyrus* genus)
Many species and varieties

Apple: The leading fruit tree in the Northwest and the nation. Earliest recorded history calls apples the "gift of the gods." Apple trees are easily identified by their characteristic round fruit known technically as a pome — a fleshy fruit having seeds borne within papery cells at the core. There are about 30 to 55 species of apple trees and several thousand varieties. Apple leaves are oval, mostly pointed at the tip and rounded at the base, soft in texture, and dull in color. The large, showy flowers are borne in clusters. Apple seeds are spread by animals and birds so that trees frequently escape to fence rows, abandoned fields and even cutover forest land.

Crab apple: Crab apples resemble common apple trees except in size. They're usually stiff, low branching, and have multiple trunks. From the great number of varieties have come some of the most valuable ornamental trees in use today. Their branches are

PHOTO: LYNN KETCHUM, © OREGON STATE UNIVERSITY
Apple

wreathed in blooms (white to red) so thick the foliage is difficult to see. Leaves may range in color from bright green to red or purple. Crab apple fruits are small and very sour; they range in color from red to orange to yellow. Birds love them, especially in winter when other food is limited.

Crab apple

Basswood *Tilia* spp. • several species

North Americans call this tree basswood, but most others call it linden; Britons often call them lime trees, although they are not related to the citrus fruit. There are about 30 species of *Tilia* in the northern hemisphere, most in Europe and Asia. Basswoods are easily recognized by their unique "ribbon leaf," from which hangs a cluster of hard, pea-size fruits on a long, thin stalk. Small white flowers produce fragrant nectar that attracts bees. Basswoods have heart-shaped leaves with uneven bases; they are about 4 to 6 inches long. It's not uncommon for basswood leaves to have tiny, bright red spires on the upper leaf surface, a result of insects laying their eggs inside the leaf.

Basswood

Birch *Betula* spp. • several species

Birch is a medium-sized genus with about 30 to 60 species, most growing in cool temperate regions of the Northern Hemisphere. Birches with white, peeling bark are the most common ornamentals; several species of white-bark birches are marketed together under the name of European white birch. The differences between them are minor. Most have bright white bark similar to our native paper birch, but none peels to the same extent. All have typical birch fruits — long, papery cones that disintegrate at maturity. Most have droopy branches that drop resin on anything that's under them. All are popular ornamental trees and tend to be planted in clumps. Not all birches have white bark — some lean toward yellow, orange, red, or black. Most have peeling bark, but this, too, can vary.

Birches in the Northwest (and almost everywhere else in North America) are commonly attacked by the bronze birch borer. This native insect lays its eggs in the bark and its larvae tunnel into the phloem for food and overwintering. Once their tunnels surround the tree, death of the tree soon follows. Dead top branches are one of the first clues. Then look for the beetles' D-shaped holes.

PHOTO: STEPHEN WARD, © OREGON STATE UNIVERSITY
Birch

Buckeye or horse-chestnut
Aesculus spp. • several species

Two common names for the same tree: buckeye because its reddish-brown seed with a huge white dot looks like a buck's eye; and horse-chestnut because its fruit is so similar to true chestnuts. Ohio's nickname, the Buckeye State, comes from a common eastern species. All buckeyes have large, palmately compound leaves, the only common tree in North America to have this characteristic. The large brown nuts are packaged in a leathery husk that may or may not have spiny bristles, depending on species. These husks split open cleanly, along straight lines. The flowers range from white to deep pink, resemble the head of an elephant, and come in huge, upright clusters, making this one of our most spectacular ornamental trees. All parts of this tree are TOXIC TO HUMANS and should not be eaten.

Buckeye or horse-chestnut

Catalpa *Catalpa* spp. • two species

Catalpas are noted for their spectacular summer flower displays. Their white, trumpet-shaped flowers grow in huge, upright clusters covering the entire tree. Each flower has a yellow nectar guide to help bees find their pollen; when the pollen is gone, the nectar guide turns red and becomes invisible to bees. The flowers develop into long, thin pods resembling 12- to 18-inch-long string beans. Catalpa leaves are also spectacular: huge and heart-shaped. Two species of catalpas are native to the southeastern United States but are commonly planted as ornamentals in the Northwest.

Catalpa

Cherry, peach, plum, apricot, almond
Prunus spp. • many species

Because of the commercial importance of each of its members, this genus has several common names, depending on which member is under consideration. For this reason, it's often easiest to use the scientific name, *Prunus*, when referring to the entire genus.

Cherry: Commonly grown for both the flowers and the fruit. Many varieties are available; some are hard to distinguish from one another. Cherry flowers are showy, creamy white to deep rose, and are borne in dense clusters. Some are fragrant, others are not. Some have a single ring of petals while others have multiple rings.

PHOTO: STEPHEN WARD, © OREGON STATE UNIVERSITY
Cherry

Fruits may be red, yellow, or black; they are most commonly round. Some are delectable; others are bitter. The bark of many cherry trees is thin, reddish-brown, and peels away from the trunk in horizontal strips. Branches have spur shoots and prominent lenticels (pores in the bark).

Several varieties of Japanese flowering cherry trees are widely planted in the Northwest. Their breathtaking flower displays are as eagerly anticipated along our streets as they are in Washington, D.C., where a gift of 2,000 cherry trees was received in 1912 from Tokyo, Japan — their descendants continue to delight people to this day.

Plum: Some are grown for their fruit, others for their flowers and foliage. Plum trees come from three continents: Europe, Asia and North America. They have attractive white or pink flowers borne in dense clusters. Fruits range from almost black through shades of red, purple, blue, green, yellow, and white. Plum trees commonly have finely toothed leaves with small glands on their petioles; some varieties have thorns. Our best-known eating plum is the Italian prune plum, though many others are grown. Several types of flowering plum trees are grown in the Northwest, especially 'Pissardi' and 'Bliriana', noted for their pink flowers and purple leaves.

Peach: Introduced to America from China in the 16th century. The tree is twiggy with slender limbs. The pink flowers are solitary and appear before the leaves. Peach trees are shorter (generally under 20 feet) and rounder than apple and pear trees. Dozens of varieties are known, including red-, yellow-, and white-flesh types; some have purple leaves and double flowers and are planted as ornamentals. The nectarine is a smooth-skinned relative of the peach.

Peach

Apricot: Similar to other members of the genus, but the trees can be distinguished by broad, sharp-pointed leaves and round, bright yellow fruits. The flowers are about 1 inch across, are pink to nearly white, and appear very early each spring. The flesh of the fruit breaks free from the inner stone, which is flattened and smooth.

Almond: At first glance, the fruit of this tree does not seem to fit its genus. Its outer covering is a hard, green husk, equivalent to the fleshy part of a cherry or plum. Inside is a double-layered seed, equivalent to a cherry or plum "pit." The outer part is semi-woody and filled with holes; this is the part that we crack and throw away. Inside is a meaty seed — the almond we eat.

Almond

Chestnut: American chestnut
Castanea dentata

There are eight or nine species of chestnut in the world. American chestnut is native to the eastern United States. It reaches over 100 feet tall and up to 10 feet in diameter. It has simple, glossy leaves up to 10 inches long; the margins of the leaves are lined with large, inwardly curving teeth. They are more than three times as long as

Chestnut leaf

they are wide and are green on both sides. Two to four smooth, brown nuts are found inside a very prickly burr, which breaks open around Halloween. The sweet, edible nuts must be roasted for maximum enjoyment.

Although American chestnut was once a dominant tree in forests of eastern North America, a virulent blight accidentally introduced from Asia swept through the forests in the early 1900s, killing nearly every chestnut tree in its path. As a result, American chestnuts are no longer commonly planted; however, a great deal of research is taking place to try to reestablish them, both in the forest and for ornamental purposes, using crosses from the few resistant plants that survived the blight. Chestnuts that are native to Europe (Spanish chestnuts) and Asia (Chinese chestnuts) are widely planted for fruit production. They both resemble American chestnut and are sometimes planted here.

Chestnut

Dogwood *Cornus* spp. • several species

Dogwoods are small, deciduous trees noted for beautiful flowers in the spring and small, bright red fruits in the fall; there are 30 to 60 species worldwide, and many varieties. Although the Northwest has its own species of dogwood, many species of non-native dogwoods are planted for ornamental purposes — both for disease resistance and for their different flowering patterns. People love the showy "flowers" of dogwoods, which are actually sets of petal-like bracts surrounding a tight, rounded head of many tiny petal-less flowers. Most North American dogwoods are susceptible to a fungus called *Anthracnose,* which results in death of branches and then entire trees. As a result, several species of eastern Asian dogwoods have gained favor recently because they're more resistant to *Anthracnose.*

White or pink flowering dogwood *(Cornus florida)*: Two varieties within the same species, one with white flowers and one with pink-to-red flowers. The main white-flowered variety is the more widespread of the two, occupying the eastern half of the U.S.; the pink-flowered variety is more common in the southeastern states. Other than flower color, they resemble each other — simple, deciduous, opposite leaves and a tightly clustered flower head surrounded by four to six showy bracts. They both resemble our Pacific dogwood.

Flowering dogwood

Kousa dogwood *(Cornus kousa)*: Kousa dogwood is one of the most popular of the Asian dogwoods. It has white-to-greenish-white petal-like bracts, although there are also pink and variegated varieties. Its bracts are more pointed than its American cousins, and there are typically only four of them surrounding a head of tiny, petal-less flowers. It flowers several weeks later than its American cousins, and only after its leaves have emerged.

Kousa dogwood fruit

Elm *Ulmus* spp. • several species

Elm leaves

Elms make lovely ornamental trees, with broad, spreading crowns that cast dense shade. As a result, they are commonly planted along Northwest streets, yards and gardens. There are 30-40 species worldwide, with some hybridizing.

American elm *(Ulmus americana):* A large tree of unforgettable form, American elm resembles the spray of a fountain or a vase overflowing with flowers. It grows naturally throughout the eastern United States and is especially prominent in New England, where it was an important forest tree. American elms were once planted in most Northwestern cities as shade trees, but

American elm

seldom are anymore because they're susceptible to Dutch elm disease, which is almost always lethal and has killed most American elms in the eastern states. Know American elm by its form; its lopsided, double-toothed leaf; and its round, flat, gauzy winged fruit (called a samara).

Siberian elm *(Ulmus pumila):* Siberian elm is a tough, hardy tree native to temperate and semi-arid regions of central Asia. Because it withstands extreme temperatures and tough environmental conditions it has been transplanted all over the world where tough trees are needed to provide shelter from harsh environmental conditions. That's how it found its way to the arid central and eastern portions of Oregon and Washington. However, it is a short-lived tree (often less than 75 years old) and it loses branches throughout its life, making it a messy ornamental for yards. Another downside is that it is highly invasive, rapidly spreading along stream channels. As a result, it is seldom planted anymore.

Ginkgo *Ginkgo biloba*

Ginkgo fruit

Ginkgo has broad leaves but is more closely related to conifers than to other broadleaves because its seeds don't develop inside ovaries. *Biloba* is the only surviving species of a larger genus that once spread multiple species across the world. Long gone from its native Asian forests, ginkgo is considered sacred by the Chinese and was saved from extinction only by

Gingko

cultivation in temple gardens. Only females of this species bear fruit, a fleshy, foul-smelling, plumlike fruit with a single seed inside; as a result, male trees are more desirable as ornamentals. Ginkgos often are planted because of their unique leaves — leaves with fan-shaped veins that turn brilliant yellow in the fall — and their toughness in the face of pollution and poor environmental conditions. In fact, ginkgos are so tough that six trees actually survived the atomic bomb blasts in Japan near the end of World War II. Although the fruit has an obnoxious smell (similar to vomit), both the fruit and leaves are used in traditional Asian medicine. The genus name, *Ginkgo*, refers to "silver apricot" while species name, *biloba*, refers to its two-lobed leaves.

Hawthorn *Crataegus* spp. • many species

Hawthorn, also called haw or thornapple, especially in Europe, is perhaps the only tree with both conspicuous woody thorns and leaves that are pinnately lobed and serrated. The flowers resemble small roses, followed by clusters of small, apple-like fruit (haws) which are edible but quite seedy and not particularly flavorful. Hundreds of species of this group of small trees grows throughout the world. The Northwest has two native species, Columbia and black hawthorn (described earlier in this book). English haw (also called one-seeded hawthorn) is the most commonly cultivated form. Its leaf is usually five-lobed and its flowers may be pink, red or white. Birds eat its red fruits (pomes) and spread its seeds widely. As a result, it is deemed highly invasive. In China, candied hawthorn fruits are considered a special treat and are served on a stick at many markets.

Hawthorn

Hazel: filbert or common hazel

Corylus avellana

Filbert is a Eurasian relative of our native California hazel. It's a small, deciduous tree easily recognized both in winter and summer. In winter it bears long, male catkins that shed yellow pollen between December and March. Female flowers resemble a large bud with several red whiskers sticking out from the end. "Filbert" is supposed to mean "full beard," referring to the husk covering the nut. Dozens of varieties are known. Nuts vary from round to oblong and from ¼ to 1 inch in diameter. Each nut is enclosed in a leafy "basket" called an involucre. Oregon produces 99% of the nation's filbert crop, marketing them as hazelnuts.

PHOTO: STEPHEN WARD, © OREGON STATE UNIVERSITY

Hazelnut

Hazelnut catkins (left) and nuts

Holly *Ilex* spp. • several species

Holly trees are long-lived and grow on all continents except Australia. There are hundreds of species, hybrids and varieties. Although none is native to the Northwest, English holly, *Ilex aquifolium,* is commonly grown in commercial orchards for Christmas sprays and wreaths. Holly is easy to identify by spike-tipped, shiny, evergreen leaves and bright red berries. Holly bears male and female flowers on separate trees, so only some trees produce fruits. English holly ranges from 20 to 40 feet tall; branches extend to the ground. Some variegated forms have white or silver margins and even, smooth-edged leaves. Hollies are aggressive invaders, as birds carry their seeds far and wide.

Holly

Honeylocust *Gleditsia triacanthos*

Seed pods

Honeylocust

Although this sounds like a type of locust tree (*Robinia*), it's actually a separate genus (*Gleditisia*); this is why the common name is either written as one word or hyphenated. Honeylocusts may have both singly-pinnate and doubly-pinnate compound leaves arising from the same twigs; singly compound leaves typically arise early in the growing season while doubly compound leaves arise later in the season; some twigs bear both forms. Doubly pinnate means that there are sets of compound leaves arising from the stems of compound leaves where normally only a single leaflet would occur.

Honeylocusts have long (8 to 18 inches), brown seed pods that are flat and twisted (the pods of true locust trees are much shorter and are straight rather than twisted). Inside the pods are hard, shiny brown seeds that shake like rattles when the pods are ripe. Native honeylocusts have long, sharp thorns, sometimes arising in a compound fashion with thorns arising from thorns, but most ornamental varieties are bred not to have them. Honeylocusts are native to the eastern United States. Trees are fast growing with an upright trunk and spreading branches, and they cast a light shade due to their small leaves; this makes them a favored shade tree.

Locust: Black locust
Robinia pseudoacacia

Black locust is native to the central Appalachian region and the Ozark Highlands of the eastern U.S. Settlers took black locusts all over the United States because they loved the fragrant, sweet-pea flowers and because of its tolerance of harsh growing conditions. Often it was the only tree that would survive the harsh conditions of the American West. In the Pacific Northwest, it was commonly planted east of the Cascades, where its resistance to heat, cold and drought made it especially useful.

Black locust

Black locust is distinguished by pinnately compound leaves (never doubly compound); two short, wickedly sharp spines at the base of each leaf; and flat, brown seed pods about 2 to 4 inches long. With sunlight shining through them, the leaves are said by some to show the most beautiful green of any broadleaf. Black locust grows rapidly to a height of 75 feet and is commonly used in windbreaks. Its wood is very durable even without treatment and was traditionally used for fence posts and railroad ties.

Black locust "fixes" nitrogen from the air and is, therefore, often used to help replenish the soil brought to the surface during strip mining operations. However, it is an aggressive, invasive species, spreading by seeds, by stump sprouts, and by root sprouts — characteristics that make it a poor choice for an ornamental tree. 'Purple Robe' is a relatively new variety of black locust, noted for its striking clusters of purple flowers. It is a medium-size tree that tolerates harsh sites, but has all the drawbacks of black locust, so don't plant it unless you're willing to keep it in check.

Locust leaf and flower of 'Purple Robe'

Maple *Acer* spp. • many species

Dozens of maple species thrive in the mild climate of western Oregon and Washington. Only a few are mentioned here. Almost all maples have opposite leaves and dry-seeded fruits (samaras) shaped like airplane propellers.

Boxelder *(Acer negundo):* Native and widespread in most states east of the Rockies, in the southern Rockies, and in central California, boxelder is such a good colonizer that it has naturalized almost everywhere in North America, including Oregon and Washington. Even where it is a native species, it is commonly described as weedy and invasive. Boxelder breaks one of the key rules for being a maple: rather than simple leaves, it almost always has pinnately compound leaves with three to seven leaflets, and occasionally produces simple leaves on the same tree. Like other maples, its seeds are paired samaras, although these have incurved wings and hang in long, dangling clusters. Its invasive nature makes it a poor choice as an ornamental.

Norway maple *(Acer platanoides):* A native of Europe that shades many Northwestern streets and lawns. It resembles our native bigleaf maple, but neither its leaves nor its size are nearly as large. Norway and bigleaf are the only maples whose leaf stems contain milky juice. Schwedler's maple, a smaller variety of Norway maple, has rich, dark red leaves that make it an important ornamental; of course, its leaves contains the green chlorophyll needed to photosynthesize, but its green color is masked by the red-purple pigment.

Silver maple *(Acer saccharinum):* A widely planted shade tree native to the eastern United States. Its leaves are cut with deep indentations and show a silvery-white color underneath. Silver maple has a wide-spreading form with the trunk dividing near the ground into big, mostly upright limbs. It is rapidly growing but short lived. It tends to shed dead branches more easily than other maples and is subject to damage from ice, wind and snow. This limits its value as an ornamental.

Sugar maple

Red maple   Norway maple

Red maple *(Acer rubrum):* Native to the eastern United States. It is a widely planted shade tree because of rapid growth, uniform shape, and leaves that turn brilliant red in the fall. It also tolerates the wet soils so common in western portions of the Pacific Northwest. It is easy to distinguish from other maples because its leaves have only three lobes. Its wood is soft and the tree splits easily in the wind and snow; not especially good traits in an ornamental tree.

Japanese maples: A large group of small trees and shrubs widely planted as ornamentals because they come in a variety of sizes and shapes. Their leaves are also different from most maples — most are deeply and narrowly lobed; many are described as being starlike. As with all maples, their leaves are opposite, and their fruits are double samaras.

Japanese maple

Mountain-ash

Sorbus spp. • many species and varieties

Berry-like fruits

Although two species of mountain-ash grow at high elevations in the Northwest, they are shrubs rather than trees. However, many nonnative species do grow as small trees — and they're commonly chosen to adorn our streets and yards. Mountain-ashes are popular ornamentals because of their vibrant colored fruits: red, yellow and orange. The small, apple-like clusters are a favorite of birds and small mammals, especially in winter when other food is scarce. Their leaves are pinnately compound and alternate (similar to true ashes, except that ash leaves are arranged oppositely), with many small leaflets; most turn yellow to orange to bright red in the crisp fall air. Mountain-ashes have the ability to grow in tight spaces, making them a favorite for storefronts and shopping centers. The hyphen in the common name tells us this is not a true ash, which reside in the genus *Fraxinus*.

Mountain-ash

Oak *Quercus* spp. • many species

There are approximately 600 species of oaks in the world, and approximately 100 in North America. The Pacific Northwest has only three native species, but many species from other parts of the world are planted here as street and lawn trees. Most are classified as red oaks because their leaves have pointed lobes ending in several bristle tips. Those with rounded lobes and no bristle tips are called white oaks. All oaks have acorns for fruits. Many species of California oaks (commonly called live oaks) have small, evergreen leaves, but few of those are planted in the Northwest.

Northern red oak *(Quercus rubra)* and scarlet oak *(Quercus coccinea):* Both are native to the eastern United States and are so similar that identification is challenging. Both are large, spreading trees that sport

Northern red oak

blazing red fall colors. Their leaves are 3 to 6 inches long and have five to nine bristle-tipped lobes. Although the leaves of each species are quite variable, those of scarlet oak tend to have deeper lobes than those of northern red oak.

Pin oak *(Quercus palustris)*: a large oak of the eastern United States that can often be recognized by its outline alone. Its upper branches point up, its middle branches spread horizontally, and its lower branches droop until they sweep the ground. Short, pin-like shoots cluster along the branches, giving the tree the name of pin oak. The glowing red-bronze autumn foliage and handsome winter form are especially attractive. Pin oak tends to hold dead leaves well into winter. It has deeply cut leaves, 3 to 5 inches long, and ½-inch-long acorns topped by flat caps.

Pin oak

Oleaster: Russian-olive *Elaeagnus angustifolia*

Russian-olive leaves

Russian-olive is a large shrub or small, bushy tree native to central and western Asia. Its branches are sometimes thorny and sometimes not. It's popular for its handsome, silvery foliage, its fragrant, pale yellow flowers, its fast growth, and its adaptability to a wide range of growing conditions. Leaves are willow-like, 1 to 3 inches long with silvery, scaly undersides. Fruits are small, one-seeded and mealy. Leaves, twigs, flowers and fruits are all touched with silver. It is commonly planted throughout the arid West, including Oregon and Washington, but it is very invasive and soon establishes colonies of its own, especially along waterways.

Russian-olive

Pear *Pyrus* spp. • many species and varieties

Fall color

Like domesticated apple trees, pear trees come to us from western Europe, northern Africa, and much of Asia; pears are not native to North America. They commonly grow strong and upright, sometimes reaching 50 feet or more. Pear leaves are simple, alternate and deciduous; they are oval to oblong, borne on short spurs, and with indistinct vein patterns. Pear fruit varies from round to oblong but always has an inner core containing brown seeds, similar to apples. White flowers appear in dense clusters and are attractive enough that nonfruiting varieties are commonly planted as ornamentals. Over 1,000 varieties have been named, but only half a dozen are grown commercially. Oregon is a leading producer of pears.

Callery pear

Poplar and cottonwood

Two names for members of the same genus, *Populus*

Lombardy poplar leaf

Lombardy or black poplar (*Populus nigra* var. *italica*): Lombardy poplar is easily identified by its slim, columnar shape — like an exclamation point rising from the landscape. Close up, you can note its up-pointing branches and triangular leaves with slender, flattened leaf stalks, making them flutter in the wind. Lombardy poplars are all male trees — that is, they do not produce seeds. Instead, they're propagated by cuttings, a process that results in genetically identical trees called clones. Because of their narrow growth form and similar growth rates, Lombardy poplars are frequently used for tall hedges and windbreaks and to line streets and roads. However, they do have drawbacks: their wood is weak and prone to breakage, and the roots disrupt sidewalks and sewer lines. Because of this, their planting is banned in some communities.

White poplar (*Populus alba*): White poplar is native to most of Europe into central Asia. It is a medium-sized deciduous tree easily identified by 5-lobed leaves (2 to 6 inches long) that are bright, downy white on their undersides. Bark on younger trees is greenish white with distinct black, raised diamonds on its surface. Introduced into the U.S. in 1748, it rapidly escaped cultivation and now grows in at least 43 states. It is considered weedy and invasive.

Underside of white poplar leaves

Sweetgum *Liquidambar styraciflua*

Sweetgum fruit

Sweetgum is native to the southeastern United States, but is one of the Northwest's most common shade and street trees. It's easily identified by its five- to seven-pointed leaves that suggest stars. Two other features that help identify it: twigs that develop thick, corky ridges, and fruit that is a peculiar, spiny ball. The fruit, about the size of a golf ball, hangs on the tree well into winter. When fall weather is

Sweetgum leaves

favorable, sweetgum's parade of color is unsurpassed. We say "parade" because one bright color follows another — scarlet, orange, wine, yellow and purple . Entire streets in western Oregon and Washington are often lined with sweetgums. One of their main drawbacks is that they are subtropical trees, and often break under heavy wet snow and wet, rainy winds.

Sycamore *Platanus spp.* • *several species*

North Americans call these trees sycamores, but the rest of the world calls them planetrees. Several species are planted in the Northwest as street and shade trees, but they're similar enough to be described together. Sycamores are easy to recognize because they shed their greenish-gray outer bark to reveal chalky, light patches of inner bark, and because their fruits are 1-inch spiny balls of tiny, tufted seeds that hang on long threads. As these seeds ripen, they fall away from the small inner ball to which they were attached. Their leaves are often referred to as "maplelike" because they are palmately lobed like maples, but sycamore leaves are alternate rather than opposite. Sycamore leaves also have a swollen stem that covers the next year's bud. Sycamores are sometimes called "ghost of the forest" because their white, patchy bark contrasts with the darkness of the understory.

Sycamore

Walnut *Juglans* spp. • several species

About 20 species of walnuts grow worldwide; the two most common walnuts grown in the Northwest are black walnut and English walnut. Sometimes two or more species are grafted together to enhance nut production. Large, pinnately compound leaves; large, hard-shelled nuts; and twigs with chambered or segmented piths are all distinctive walnut characteristics.

Nut

Black walnut *(Juglans nigra)*: develops an immense, rounded crown and may grow to 150 feet tall and many feet in diameter. It is easy to recognize by its long, pinnately compound leaves (up to 24 inches long with 15 to 20 leaflets) and its hard, black, deeply grooved nut. Leaves and nuts both have distinctive, penetrating odors. You can extract the nuts (with great difficulty) to furnish a delicious nut for ice cream, candies and baked goods. The shells are so hard that in the past they were added to rubber tires and asphalt to make them last longer. Limbs are larger, darker and rougher than those of other walnuts.

Black walnut leaf

English walnut leaf

English walnut *(Juglans regia)*: Nuts are smoother and shells are thinner than those of black walnut, making them far easier to crack. Also, their leaves have fewer (generally five to seven) and larger leaflets than black walnut. But the twig piths are still chambered. This species actually originated in Asia rather than England but was distributed and popularized by the English several centuries ago. Leaves, twigs and fruit hulls have a strong odor and can stain your hands brown.

Willow *Salix* spp. • many species

There are some 400 species of willow in the world, and many more varieties and hybrids. Many species of willow are native to the Pacific Northwest, but still more have been introduced for ornamental purposes. Only two common ones will be described here.

Weeping willow *(Salix babylonica)*: Best known for its narrow leaves and drooping, whiplike branches. Dense, ropelike branches, on this medium-size tree (60 to 80 feet) present an attractive winter design. Voracious roots reach far to foul up drains. Ropes and baskets from willow slips must have been among the earliest known manufactured articles of humans. Originally from China, weeping willow is now widely planted across temperate regions of the world.

Golden willow *(Salix alba var. vitellina)*: Less drooping, less dense and less invasive than weeping willow. Bright orange branches make it attractive in winter. Widely adaptable to soil and moisture conditions, it's frequently seen in eastern Oregon and Washington, where it can be used in windbreaks.

Weeping willow

Yellow-poplar or tulip-poplar

Liriodendron tulipifera

Flower

Fruit

Yellow-poplar is native to the eastern United States, where it grows fast, tall and straight, and loses its bottom branches, similar to many conifers — making it an important commercial forest tree. There are many ways to recognize this tree. Leaves are simple, alternate and deciduous with 4 distinct lobes (resulting in an unusual squarish shape). Flowers resemble green tulips with a broad orange band around them, but you have to look closely to find them as they bloom after the leaves. Winter buds are shaped like a duck's bill. Fruits are multiple samaras borne upright in a cup-shaped manner; when ripe the samaras fall away from the spike holding them together, leaving the spike to bear the brunt of winter weather. Yellow-poplar is important both as a forest tree in the eastern U.S. and for landscaping across the Northwest and in many temperate regions of the northern hemisphere. The hyphen in the common name tells us this is not a true poplar (*Populus* spp.)

Yellow-poplar

Giant tree ferns approaching the size of trees probably made up the Earth's first "forests."

Yesterday and today

Oregon and Washington are two of our most diverse states, whether we consider their geography, their climate, or their forests. Environments range from cool, wet coastal lands to towering, snow-capped mountains, to hot, parched semi-arid rangelands, to cold deserts that may receive only 5 inches of rain a year. Forests occupy approximately half of the total land base of Oregon and Washington — over 50 million acres. They include majestic stands of Douglas-fir and western hemlock in the Coast and Cascade ranges, snow-stunted spruce and fir forests near timberline, and open, parklike stands of pine and juniper east of the Cascades.

But it was not always so. In the distant past, long before people first roamed the continent, even before the mountains were formed, Northwest forests were radically different from those of today.

Tree ferns and horsetails give way to towering giants

Ralph E. Duddles, Allan Campbell III and Lou Torres
Adapted in 2020 by Edward C. Jensen

Four hundred million years ago, the Pacific Northwest, like much of North America, was a warm, swampy place. Giant tree ferns and horsetails lined the swamps and probably formed our first "forests." Although these ferns and horsetails reached the size of trees, they were not true trees: Their stems were not woody, and they did not produce annual rings.

About 200 million years ago, the first primitive trees — conifers, ginkgos, and cycads — began to develop. They probably grew on large islands within vast inland seas.

When the extensive chain of mountains now called the Rockies began to form about 70 million years ago, the North American West began a slow drying-out process that stimulated the development of land plants. The climate and forests of the Northwest became subtropical, dominated by trees such as palms, figs, laurels, avocados, cinnamon and dawn redwood (a primitive conifer currently native only to China).

Over time, these subtropical plants gradually disappeared from the Northwest, and our forests began to resemble those that now grow in the eastern half of North America — a mixture of maples, oaks, basswoods, elms, and sycamores, as well as a host of conifers that now grow only in eastern Asia.

About 13 million years ago, the Cascade Mountains and the Coast Ranges of Oregon and Washington began to rise from the swampy sea, dramatically changing the climate of the Northwest. Annual rainfall was drastically reduced east of the Cascades, and temperature began to fluctuate more widely. Subtropical trees disappeared.

The survivors were trees that could tolerate cold winters and prolonged drought, such as aspens, spruces and pines. In the western, more temperate side of the Northwest, willows, cottonwoods, cherries and maples flourished. About 1 million years ago, the forests began to resemble those of today.

Then came the ice. Massive glaciers pushed down from the north and through the valleys emanating from the Cascades and other mountain ranges. The effect on the land was profound, as the moving rivers of ice completely destroyed entire forests. Most of the Northwest's forests are still recovering from the last glacial period, which ended almost 10,000 years ago.

Through time, prolonged dryness became a dominant part of Northwest weather patterns. Recurring summer drought and wildfire emerged as significant factors in the evolution of our forests. Fires' severity and frequency — along with other disturbances such as flooding, windthrow, and the impacts of humans — have had a dramatic effect on the forests we see today.

About 13 million years ago, the Cascade Mountains and the Coast Ranges of Oregon and Washington began to rise from the swampy sea.

Forests meet the horizon in the Dungeness River Valley, Olympic National Forest, Washington.

Northwest forests today

David A. Zahler and Edward C. Jensen

Today, the forests of Oregon and Washington are among the most diverse, productive and magnificent in the world. They range from dry, open juniper- and pine-dominated forests east of the Cascades to wet, majestic old-growth Douglas-fir and western hemlock forests west of the Cascades. They blanket most of western Oregon and Washington and all but the highest mountain peaks and driest plains and valleys of the central and eastern regions of the two states. Although most of our forests are dominated by needle-leaved conifers, many species of hardwoods play important ecological roles. Nearly all tree species that grow in our forests achieve their largest size and reach their oldest age here.

Although the percentage of Oregon and Washington occupied by forests hasn't changed much in the past 200 years, the structure, composition and distribution of our forests have changed dramatically. Most forests of the early 1800s have been removed by fire, logging and other disturbances. They were replaced with native trees, but in mixes different from the original ones. Some old-growth forests remain, mostly in remote parts of public lands. Many low-elevation forests have been lost to agricultural and urban development, although many communities now try to preserve remaining stands.

East of the Cascades, juniper woodlands have expanded significantly due to control of wildfires. Fire suppression has created many other changes. Given the types and extent of change over time, much of modern forestry is directed at maintaining the health and diversity of Northwest forests while producing the wood, water, wildlife and recreation that society demands.

Douglas-fir forests

Douglas-fir forests are the most extensive type of forests in Oregon and Washington; they're also the most important for timber production. Although Douglas-fir is the dominant forest tree west of the Cascade crest, it's also an important component of eastside forests.

West of the Cascades, Douglas-fir often forms vast, nearly pure stands, a result of both natural conditions and human management. Common associated species include western hemlock (the climax species for much of this region), western redcedar, noble fir, bigleaf maple and red alder (the most common early successional species for most of this region).

East of the Cascades, where forests are drier, common associates of Douglas-fir include incense-cedar, sugar pine, western white pine, ponderosa pine, grand fir, white fir and western larch, depending on moisture and stand history.

Understories (the combined set of species growing beneath the tree canopy) vary from dense to sparse depending on the availability of moisture, but are generally rich in shrubs and herbs.

Douglas-fir is a long-lived, early- to mid-successional species. This means that it is among the first species to invade disturbed sites, but it can continue to dominate these sites for hundreds of years

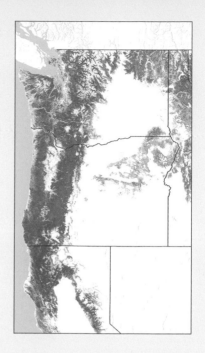

Douglas-fir dominates forests west of the Cascades, where it can live for hundreds of years.

before it eventually is replaced by more shade-tolerant species, such as western hemlock. More often than not, a major disturbance such as a catastrophic fire or windstorm prevents those climax forests of western hemlock from developing, resetting the successional clock to favor Douglas-fir.

Douglas-fir forests grow under a wide variety of conditions. The climate of westside Douglas-fir forests ranges from wet and mild in the north to drier and warmer in the south. Eastside Douglas-fir forests are much drier than those of western Oregon and Washington and have more extreme temperature fluctuations, both daily and seasonally.

Prior to human management, Douglas-fir forests originated following large disturbances such as fire, landslides and windstorms. Sometimes, Douglas-fir recolonized the sites rapidly, resulting in relatively even-aged stands; sometimes it took much longer, resulting in uneven-aged stands in which the dominant trees vary significantly in age.

Although Douglas-fir trees become commercially valuable around age 30, time between harvests can range from 30 to 100 years (or more), depending on management objectives. Over most of the westside, timber management practices such as clearcutting and shelterwood harvests are followed by planting and thinning, resulting in even-aged forests.

In drier areas like southwestern and eastern Oregon, management practices commonly include individual-tree and small-group-selection harvests that result in uneven-aged stands.

Sitka spruce and western hemlock forests

Forests dominated by western hemlock and Sitka spruce hug the fog belt along the coast of Oregon and Washington, seldom reaching more than a few miles inland or a few hundred feet above sea level. Both species tolerate shade, but Sitka spruce is more resistant to salt spray.

Sitka spruce sometimes grows in pure stands but more commonly is mixed with western hemlock, western redcedar, Douglas-fir, red alder and lodgepole pine (commonly called shore pine along the coast).

Near the California border, Port-Orford-cedar, Oregon-myrtle (also called California-laurel), and coast redwood join the mix.

Understories are typically dense with shrubs, ferns, herbs and epiphytes such as mosses and lichens. Hemlock and spruce seedlings often establish on rotting tree logs called "nurse logs." Straight lines of trees originally established on the same nurse log are common in old, undisturbed forests.

The climate of this zone is wet and mild; both daily and annual temperature fluctuations are modest. Frequent, dense summer fog helps limit the evaporative power of the sun, while fog that condenses on tree crowns adds greatly to soil moisture through fog drip.

These forests are among the most productive in the world. Historically, spruce–hemlock forests were clear-cut and replanted with Douglas-fir, a more commercially valuable species — both for its growth rate and the properties of its wood. Douglas-fir plantations were commonly invaded by western hemlock, Sitka spruce and red alder, resulting in mixed stands.

Recently a needle disease called Swiss needle cast has caused managers to reconsider when and where to plant Douglas-fir. Thinning is a key to maintaining the productivity and vigor of these stands.

Western hemlock/Sitka spruce forests have traditionally provided pulp for high-quality paper; they also are managed for specialty wood products and a variety of wildlife.

A young, productive Sitka spruce stand along the Oregon Coast.

Large, old Sitka spruce growing in the Quinault Valley of Olympic National Park, Washington

Siskiyou mixed-conifer forests

The range of topography in the Klamath and Siskiyou mountain ranges of southwestern Oregon supports a diversity of forest types. Conifers like Douglas-fir and ponderosa pine live alongside Pacific madrone, tanoak, golden chinkapin and other drought-tolerant species.

PHOTO:
U.S. FOREST SERVICE

The Klamath, Siskiyou and Cascade mountains of southwestern Oregon hold a complex mix of forest types. Forests near the coast are dominated by conifers in the upper canopy and hardwoods in the lower canopy; and forests nearer the Cascades are dominated by mixed conifers, with fewer hardwoods. Relatively few stands in either area are dominated by a single species. Conifers are the commercially important species, so these forests often are lumped together as "mixed-conifer" forests, even when broadleaved trees are present.

Elevation, distance from the ocean, fire history, and past management all influence the composition of these forests. Near the coast, Douglas-fir and tanoak are the most important species. Golden chinkapin, Pacific madrone, and canyon live oak are hardwoods of secondary importance, while sugar pine, ponderosa pine, and incense-cedar are secondary conifers. Port-Orford-cedar and bigleaf maple grow on moist sites nearer the coast; Jeffrey and knobcone pines are common on serpentine soils (those high in magnesium). As elevation increases, hardwoods become less common, and grand fir and white fir join the conifer mix. Near the Cascades, forests are dominated by mixed stands of Douglas-fir, ponderosa pine, sugar pine, incense-cedar, and white fir. This is the northernmost edge of the mixed-conifer forests that dominate the Sierra Nevada Mountains of California. Throughout the mixed-conifer forests, understories are sparse and shrubby with lots of poisonoak.

Climates range from cool and moist near the coast to hot and dry

in the interior valleys. Complex topography creates a variety of microclimates that support diverse forest types. Elevation and aspect (the direction a hillside faces) play a major role in determining how much moisture is available for tree growth.

Fire is a key factor in managing these forests. Native Americans regularly burned the mixed-conifer forests; this resulted in open stands characterized by shade-intolerant trees. Recent fire suppression has increased the density of trees and dramatically raised the hazard from fire and insects (trees growing too densely are more prone to insects and diseases). A combination of thinning and fire management is crucial to return forests to healthy and productive conditions. Both even- and uneven-aged management, in which individual and small groups of trees are selected for harvest, are common management practices.

Coast redwood forests

This is the rarest forest type in the Northwest. It is the northernmost extension of the much larger redwood forest of the northern and central California coast, reaching only about 10 miles into southern Oregon. Redwood forests grow in wet, mild, maritime climates with frequent summer fog. "Fog drip" is an important source of moisture, especially in the drier summer months. In California, redwood forests are found along valley bottoms; in Oregon they are found on mountain slopes, where the trees don't grow nearly as large as their southern neighbors. Douglas-fir, tanoak, California-laurel, bigleaf maple, golden chinkapin, Sitka spruce and western hemlock are commonly found in this forest type.

Redwoods are tough trees. They tolerate shade, have thick bark that resists fire damage, have heartwood

Redwoods just barely extend into southwest Oregon.

Urban forests

By definition, urban forests lie near or within urban boundaries. These are not the forests that we escape to for the weekend; they are the forests that enrich our daily lives where we work and play. Although they sometimes include remnant stands of native forests, more often they're a mix of native and introduced trees that have been planted along streets and in parks for recreation and beauty. Without careful tending, urban forests would either perish or be overrun by native forests. As Northwest communities grow in area and population, urban forests will play an increasingly significant role in our lives.

With appropriate care, urban forests can be maintained in almost any climate. Rather than being a product of their climate, they often are valued for the microclimates they help create. Their canopies reduce air pollution, filter rainwater, and create shade that cools the city.

Trees in the urban forest increase property values, help shops attract customers, and support both resident and migratory wildlife. Some benefits of urban forests are difficult to quantify, such as their role in capturing carbon dioxide (CO_2), an important greenhouse gas, and their contribution to the cultural well-being of our communities. Many communities in the Northwest employ urban foresters; others rely on volunteers to help manage their urban forests. Management often involves caring for individual trees (arboriculture) rather than entire forests (silviculture), although some communities own and manage entire forests. Thus, community education is also an important part of urban forestry.

that repels insects and decay, and they sprout following injury or burial from flooding. Because redwoods naturally regenerate from root suckers and stumps, small groups of trees ranging from young to very old may actually be sprouts from the same individual. Individual trees can live more than 1,000 years, and stands can occupy sites almost indefinitely, regenerating themselves after disturbance.

Although approximately 382,000 acres of redwood forests are now protected by law in national, state and local parks, this represents only about 5% of the redwood acreage that existed at the start of the California gold rush in 1849. Far more acres of redwoods (about 1.2 million acres) lie outside of protected areas and are still actively managed for timber production. These forests are managed in both even- and uneven-aged stands, using both clearcutting and individual tree selection harvest techniques. The wood from these forests is extremely valuable for an array of lumber, furniture and bark products.

PHOTO: LESSA CLAYTON
Street trees in Sherwood, Oregon contribute to urban forests.

Oak woodlands once spread across the broad river valleys of western Oregon and Washington.

Hardwood forests

Washington and Oregon — but especially Oregon —
have many species of broadleaved trees (also known as
hardwoods). But generally they grow as individuals and
in small stands, rather than in expansive forests as they
do in the eastern United States. As a result, hardwood
forests in the Northwest are not uniform and widespread,
but vary by location, environment and stand history.

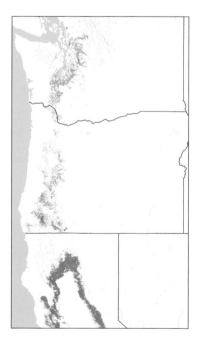

Oak woodlands, the main hardwood type in
Northwest forests, once spread across the Willamette,
Umpqua and Rogue River valleys of western Oregon. In
Washington, they extended into southern portions of
the Puget Trough, along the sun-drenched banks of the
Columbia Gorge, and northward along the eastern flanks
of the Cascades. Oregon white oak is the main species in
these woodlands, joined by bigleaf maple on wetter sites.
Moving toward southwestern Oregon, California black
oak, canyon live oak, tanoak, Pacific madrone, and golden
chinkapin become increasingly common. Before European
settlement, Northwest Indians used fire to maintain
these lands as open woodlands, but with decades of fire
suppression, many stands were invaded by more shade-
tolerant conifers such as Douglas-fir and incense-cedar.
When this happens, the conifers commonly outgrow and
shade out the oaks.

Many of these woodlands have also been lost to
agriculture, urban development and, more recently, to
vineyards.

River channels and valley bottoms (collectively
called riparian systems) throughout the Northwest are
commonly dominated by hardwoods, but the species

vary widely by location. Oregon ash, red and white alders, bigleaf maple and black cottonwood are common throughout much of western Oregon and Washington. Along the southwest coast of Oregon, California-laurel and golden chinkapin join the mix. East of the Cascades, birches, willows and cottonwoods are common. Oregon ash commonly dominates silty bottomlands where water stands during winter, while cottonwoods prefer gravelly stream banks with better drainage.

Northwestern riparian forests are getting more attention as their vital contributions to water quality and fish habitat become better understood. In the cold, dry climate east of the Cascades, picturesque groves of white-barked quaking aspen grow, often in wet meadows. Aspen is a species that produces new trees by seeds, but also by root suckers; consequently, each stand may be composed of only a few clones that spread, and grow larger, year-by-year. Wherever it grows, aspen is prized for its brilliant fall color.

The climates in which hardwood forests grow vary dramatically, from the wet, mild weather of northwestern Oregon and western Washington to the warmer, drier weather of southwestern Oregon to the highly variable seasonality of eastern Oregon and Washington. Different species of hardwoods are adapted to different environmental conditions.

Hardwood management is small in scale but growing in potential. Red alder is actively managed for wood production where it grows naturally and is commonly planted in Douglas-fir stands that are infected with root rot. Oregon white oak, Pacific madrone, bigleaf maple and Oregon ash all have attractive wood and find some use in flooring and other wood products. Black cottonwoods and non-native hybrid poplar plantations are being planted in several parts of the Northwest to help meet the demand for short-fiber pulp; some also are managed for a variety of uses including veneer and furniture.

Aspen in Ochoco National Forest, Oregon. Aspen often grows in wet meadows and along streams.

PHOTO: U.S. FOREST SERVICE

Ponderosa pine forests

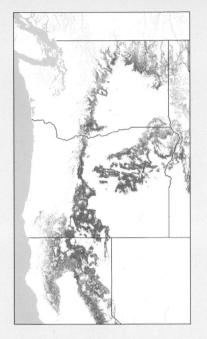

Ponderosa pine forests are widely distributed in central and eastern Oregon and Washington, ranging in elevation from 2,500 to 6,000 feet. These pines occur in pure stands or may be mixed with lodgepole pine, grand fir, Douglas-fir, western larch, western white pine, incense-cedar, white fir and quaking aspen. Volcanic pumice soils often support pure stands of ponderosa pine. Ponderosa pine is also an important component of the mixed-conifer forests of southwestern Oregon but does not form pure stands there. The Willamette Valley of western Oregon also supports a native population of ponderosa pines, especially on sites too wet for Douglas-fir (which seems odd, since eastside ponderosa forests grow on dry sites). Eastside ponderosa pine forests are the second driest forests in Oregon and Washington; they thrive in climates with short, dry summers and cold, snowy winters. The range of these forests is closely tied to soil moisture.

Fire has shaped ponderosa pine forests. Historically, frequent ground fires, both human-caused and natural, maintained open, parklike conditions. Fire suppression during the past 100 years has left many stands overcrowded with more shade-tolerant species of trees. These forests are now very susceptible to insects, disease, and fire. They can be returned to more natural and healthy conditions with a combination of thinning and prescribed fire.

Ponderosa pine forests are not typically harvested by clearcutting because removing the entire overstory can lead to extreme soil temperatures and poor natural regeneration. As a result, trees are often harvested individually or in small patches, leaving a forest with diverse structure and ages. Ponderosa pine is prized for lumber and many other uses; its color and beauty attract movie makers and recreationists alike to its photogenic forest scenes.

PHOTO : U.S. FOREST SERVICE

A ponderosa pine stand managed using prescribed fire in Oregon's Deschutes National Forest.

Lodgepole pine forests

Lodgepole pine is one of the most widely distributed trees in western North America, growing both along the Pacific Coast, where it is commonly called shore pine, and east of the Cascade crest, where it is called lodgepole pine. In the Northwest, lodgepole pine forests most commonly are associated with central and eastern Oregon and Washington, where they typically grow in pure and nearly pure stands. Throughout most of its range, lodgepole pine is an early successional species that rapidly colonizes disturbed sites, often giving way over time to more shade-tolerant species. Most lodgepole pine stands develop after fire or logging; however, they may form climax forests on sites with deep pumice and volcanic ash — too harsh for most other tree species. Lodgepole pine forests grow in dense stands that contain lots of dead trees. Stands are very susceptible to insect attacks, especially mountain pine beetle, and are frequently in danger from fire.

Lodgepole pine is an adaptable species that often flourishes where other trees cannot. Lodgepole forests are found in climates with short, dry summers and snowy winters. They commonly occur in frost pockets and on both excessively wet and dry soils.

Lodgepole pine forests typically are harvested via clearcutting, shelterwood and seed tree methods that encourage the growth of more valuable ponderosa pine. Shore pines are not managed commercially but are valued for their interesting shapes and wildlife habitat.

A lodgepole pine stand near Big Lake, high in the Oregon Cascades.

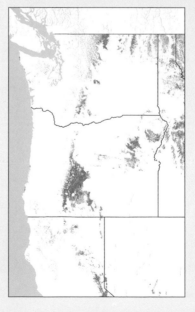

Subalpine forests

Subalpine forests are a combination of several forest types, all above 4,500 feet in the Cascades, Siskiyou and Wallowa mountains. These forests vary widely depending on stand age, fire history and local conditions. Common trees include Pacific silver fir, California red fir, noble fir, white fir, subalpine fir, western hemlock, mountain hemlock, Douglas-fir, Alaska-cedar, incense-cedar, lodgepole pine, western white pine, Engelmann spruce and quaking aspen. Many species of huckleberry grow beneath the trees and in openings caused by fire and logging.

Subalpine forests occur in cold climates with heavy winter snow packs and short growing seasons. At their upper limit, they form open, parklike forests and merge with alpine meadows. Most of these forests occur in remote areas on public land; commercial timber management is limited, and recreational values are high. Decades of fire suppression have left many stands overcrowded, diseased and stressed. Many fire ecologists believe these forests should be thinned or treated by prescribed burning to reduce fire hazard and to control insects and disease.

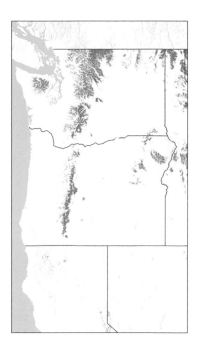

PHOTO : U.S. FOREST SERVICE

Sunrise at Paulina Peak on the Newberry National Volcanic Monument in Oregon. Subalpine forests depend on deep snowpacks, but trees must withstand heavy snow loads.

Western juniper woodlands

Three species of juniper trees (western, Rocky Mountain and California) and one species that only grows as a sprawling shrub (common juniper) are native to the Northwest. Of the trees, only western juniper is widespread, forming extensive stands in central and eastern Oregon; it is far less common in Washington. Although commonly called forests, juniper stands typically have widely-spaced, open-grown trees in which their crowns seldom touch—typical of dry woodlands. Juniper woodlands grow in areas with hot, dry summers and cold, dry winters; most precipitation falls during winter. Although Rocky Mountain juniper ranges widely across western North America, it is not common in the Northwest. California juniper is quite rare.

Due to intense competition for water and an aversion to shade, western junipers grow in open, parklike stands, interspersed with desert shrubs and grasses. Ponderosa pine may join the mix in canyons and on moist, north-facing slopes. Prior to European settlement and fire suppression, juniper woodlands were primarily limited to shallow soils and rimrock, where vegetation was too sparse to carry fire. Fire suppression has permitted western juniper to expand rapidly into traditional rangelands, where it competes with native grasses for water and nutrients. In fact, this is the only Northwestern forest type that has expanded in area occupied since the Lewis and Clark Expedition in 1804–1806. Because of this expansion, current management commonly aims to control the spread of junipers. Fire and cutting, often in combination, are used to control junipers and to stimulate the growth of native grasses.

Although the wood of western juniper is attractive, it is primarily used for minor forest products. A variety of oils and chemicals are distilled from its foliage and used commercially, and its aromatic, berrylike cones are used to flavor gin.

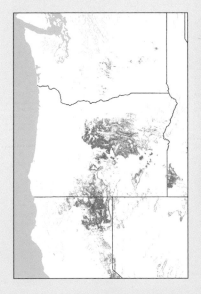

Historically, western juniper woodlands typically occurred on open, rocky sites. With fire suppression, they have expanded their range and density.

PHOTO : BILL JOHNSON/IMAGESHARP.COM

Western larch is a deciduous conifer. Stands commonly develop after fire.

Western larch forests

Western larch, one of the world's few deciduous conifers, is noted for its brilliant golden autumn colors. Rather than forming extensive forests, stands of western larch commonly develop within Douglas-fir, grand fir and ponderosa pine forests after fire or major disturbance from wind, soil movement or logging. Without periodic disturbance, larch stands eventually will be taken over by Douglas-fir on drier sites or by grand fir on milder sites. Lodgepole pine, western hemlock, western white pine and Engelmann spruce also grow in this forest type.

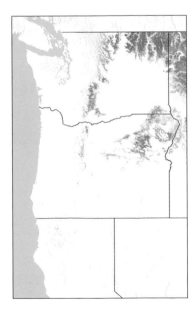

Western larch prefers cool, moist sites and depends on frequent disturbance, most commonly fire, to regenerate. Because of its intolerance to shade, western larch is managed in even-aged stands using techniques such as clearcutting, shelterwood and seed tree cuttings that encourage soil disturbance and improve chances for natural regeneration.

Controlling competing species and creating mineral seedbeds with fire is essential to maintaining western larch in forest stands. Western larch is harvested for high-quality lumber that resists decay.

People and trees: an inseparable bond

Ralph E. Duddles, Allan Campbell III and Lou Torres
Adapted in 2020 by Edward C. Jensen

Ask Northwesterners what trees and forests mean to them and you'll receive many different answers. Trees are a part of our heritage. They are a part of our lives. They have an almost spiritual importance for many of us.

Economically, trees provide a significant source of employment and revenue to citizens of Oregon and Washington. A major source of private and public employment in this two-state region comes directly or indirectly from the wood products industry. Local governments and schools in both states benefit from timber harvest revenues from both private and public lands. And many of our counties depend significantly on timber-related revenues for schools and general services such as public health, safety and roads.

Public values regarding our forests have changed dramatically in recent years. Much of the change results from significant urban growth throughout our region. While the population has changed, so have the public's views on the importance of trees. Forest products and jobs remain important cornerstones of our economy. However, an ever-increasing urban population looks to forests more for recreation, viewing wildlife, enjoying forested

Children move through Schriebers Meadow near Mount Baker in Washington. From an early age, Northwesterners develop a relationship with trees.

PHOTO:
U.S. FOREST SERVICE

wetlands, and other forest values. A growing number of Northwesterners are calling for the protection of sensitive resources such as threatened and endangered species and clear, clean water. At the same time, the income and livelihood of a significant number of our citizens depend heavily on timber production. Finding a balance or middle ground between competing ecological and economic values will continue to challenge public and private land managers in the coming years.

The forests of Oregon and Washington have always been important to the people who have lived here, even from the earliest times. Many Northwest Indian tribes chose to live along the coast, where they used the bark and wood from forest trees, especially western redcedar, for tools, fuel, clothing, canoes and plank houses. Although they valued forests as a source of raw materials, they also valued them as a home for animals and spirits that were important to their culture.

Historically, the Kalapuya Indians of the Willamette Valley annually burned the savannas to aid in gathering food, to stimulate the growth of certain species, and to make it easier to detect approaching enemies. In drier parts of the state, local Northwest Indian tribes underburned low-elevation forests to improve game habitat and hunting. These fires often escaped control, destroying large stands of trees.

Large-scale changes to Northwest forests began when settlers moved into the Oregon Territory. First came the explorers, fur trappers, adventurers — and even botanists. One such botanist was Archibald Menzies, a Scottish physician in the British Navy. In 1792, he made the first known collections of Douglas-fir (*Pseudotsuga menziesii*) and Pacific madrone (*Arbutus menziesii*). The scientific names of both trees now bear his name.

It was the Lewis and Clark Expedition (1804–1806), under the authority of President Thomas Jefferson, that pushed wide the gates to exploration and exploitation of western forest lands. Jefferson chose well in selecting Meriwether Lewis and William Clark to lead

this group. Their detailed journals provided superb written descriptions of western forests. In one entry, they wrote that "the trees of larger growth are very abundant; the whole neighborhood of the coast is supplied with great quantities of excellent timber." In another, one tree was "found to be forty-two feet in circumference," and for a "distance of two hundred feet was destitute of limbs."

Another Scottish botanist scribed an unalterable mark on the Northwest's forest history. Truly an adventurer, he traveled thousands of miles by foot, horseback, and canoe. He was David Douglas, son of a stonemason and probably the most famous figure in the history of 19th-century American botany. Between 1825 and 1834, Douglas spent over two years in the Northwest, where he first identified the giant chinkapin and many

ILLUSTRATION: J. SEMEYN, INDIAN LEGENDS OF VANCOUVER ISLAND

Native American women are depicted harvesting western redcedar bark. Historically, most clothing was made of shredded, woven bark.

PHOTO: U.S. FOREST SERVICE

Early log trucks haul old-growth Douglas-fir.

An acorn woodpecker, known for drilling holes in which to store its favorite nut.

A modern log truck hauling Douglas-fir to a mill.

different species of oak, maple, pine, fir and spruce. The common name of the Northwest's most abundant tree, Douglas-fir, honors this great adventurer.

The relationship of humans to Northwestern forests changed drastically with the arrival of significant numbers of settlers early in the 19th century. Their original interests were furs and farming, but it wasn't long before they began exploiting forests and all their resources. In the earliest stages of settlement, timber had little monetary value, but it was important to the lives of the new farmers. Houses, furniture, tools, utensils, vehicles, machinery and heat all came from wood.

The first sawmill in Oregon was built in 1842 at the falls of the Willamette River in Oregon City. Washington soon followed with the steam-powered Yesler mill in Seattle (1852). The California gold rush and the explosive growth of San Francisco made lumbering the Northwest's leading industry and set the stage for the region that we know today.

Over the years, the Northwest has seen an increasing demand for forest resources other than timber. The growing population is looking increasingly to forests for recreation, clean water, fish and wildlife, and other ecological values. Also, travel and tourism, dependent to a great extent on the region's majestic forests, play an ever-increasing role in the economies of both states.

Because of the increasing demand on our forests to fill a variety of needs, caring for our forests becomes all the more important. Much of this is accomplished through a concept called stewardship. Stewardship means providing responsible, nurturing care — for a person, a family, a business and even a forest. This caring and nurturing has allowed us to protect our forests, promote responsible forest practices and encourage a variety of forest uses. It also helps Northwesterners understand the diversity of benefits our forests offer and how our forests grow and survive.

The idea of stewardship isn't new. Most public and private forest landowners already use forest lands wisely by emphasizing a variety of management practices. The principles behind stewardship allow forest landowners to manage their lands intensively not only for better timber

growth and quality but also for better wildlife and fisheries habitat, soil protection, beauty and recreational opportunities.

As well as being biologically diverse, the Northwest's forests have diverse patterns of ownership, which greatly affects how they're managed. More than half of Oregon's forests (57%) are federally owned and managed, primarily by the U.S. Forest Service, U.S. Park Service, and the Bureau of Land Management; in Washington it's about 43%. These lands most often are managed for a variety of uses such as timber, grazing, wildlife, watershed and recreation.

But the national forests in Washington and Oregon also contain about 70 designated wilderness areas totaling approximately 6.8 million acres. These areas offer solitude and wilderness experiences that enrich and rejuvenate the spirit. The two-state region contains four national parks: Crater Lake in Oregon; and Mount Rainier, Olympic, and North Cascades in Washington, each world-renowned for the values they encompass. The National Park Service also administers six national monuments in the two-state region: Oregon Caves, John Day Fossil Beds and Fort Clatsop in Oregon; and the San Juan Islands, Mount St. Helens and Hanford Reach in Washington. Each recognizes a national landmark or historic place in the life of our country.

Industrial owners manage about 21% of forest land in each of our two states, primarily producing logs and other wood products. These lands are generally among the most productive forest lands in the Northwest. In

Mountain goats on Mount Ellinor on the Olympic National Forest, Washington.

PHOTO:
U.S. FOREST SERVICE

People look to forests for recreation, clean water and other values. Here, a paddleboarder passes a golden-hued grove on the Deschutes National Forest.

PHOTO:
U.S. FOREST SERVICE

decades before the 1990s, industrial lands accounted for nearly 40% of our annual timber harvest; more recently their share has risen to 75% to 80%, due in part to declining harvests from federal lands.

Private, nonindustrial landowners own nearly 16% of Oregon's forests, and 15% in Washington. A tremendous assortment of people fall into this category, including doctors, farmers, bankers, teachers, loggers and lawyers, to name but a few. They manage their properties for a wide variety of reasons: income, wildlife habitat, livestock grazing, mushroom production or simply to have a special place to call their own and pass on to their children.

To understand the important role of trees to Northwesterners, it helps to understand the contributions that the Forest Practices Acts have played in protecting many forest values. Oregon passed its Forest Protection Act in 1971 and

Washington followed soon after in 1974. Each was among the first in the nation to be passed and each has been reviewed and revised many times since its passage. Each Forest Practices Act is designed to protect the environment during harvesting and other forest operations. A key component of the act requires that all land be successfully reforested within two or three years of harvest. The Forest Practices Act also protects forest streams and wetlands, endangered wildlife, and designated scenic corridors. It limits clearcut size and allows for the retention of snags and green trees during forest operations. A key feature of each act is its ability to evolve over time to reflect new science and the public's changing values. Throughout their history, the two Forest Practices Acts have changed in response to new information and new concerns.

Urbanization is also a dominant human influence on Northwestern forests. The ever-increasing sprawl of housing developments, highways and shopping centers continually breaks our forests into smaller and smaller fragments. Urbanization has greatly influenced the kinds of management feasible in surrounding forests. It has fathered dramatic increases in fire hazard and destructive forest insects and diseases. Many of these increases can be traced to physical abuses of the forest environment that, in turn, stress forest trees. Soil compaction, dumping of refuse, scarring of trees and improper road location are but a few examples of the human-caused stress that impairs soil structure, forested waterways, individual standing trees and even whole forest stands.

In addition, urban growth has created new demands on forest lands to provide water, recreation and clean air. Forests once harvested to provide wood products for a growing society now are being managed to filter water for drinking, to cleanse the air for breathing, to provide trails for hiking, and, in general, to soothe our spirits. In essence, the original storehouse of raw materials encountered by early American adventurers, botanists and settlers is being reshaped to accommodate a growing nation.

Throughout history, the forests of Oregon and Washington have undergone continual change. Climatic fluctuations, volcanic eruptions, fire and exploitation by humans are just a few of the more dramatic causes. Our future — the future of Northwest forests, and the future of the Northwest's people — has been and always will be linked to adaptation and change. And regardless of the changes, forests will always play an important role in our lives.

Snowshoers traverse Bennett Pass in Mount Hood National Forest, above. At left, a trail ride in the Ochoco National Forest.

PHOTOS:
U.S. FOREST SERVICE

Northwest forests face a changing climate

Edward C. Jensen and David Shaw, OSU Extension forest health specialist

While we can debate the underlying causes, Northwest forests face a future of climate change and challenge. We can only speculate on the specific changes that may occur. But forests are resilient, and they will adapt to survive.

Perhaps it helps to remember that climate has always changed over time, and that forests have always responded. Consider that 10,000 years ago, the Puget Trough of Washington was buried under a mile of ice that scraped all underlying forests off the map! Only as the ice retreated did the forests that now occupy the land re-establish themselves in our landscape. And millions of years ago, Northwest forests resembled the warm, temperate, broadleaved forests of eastern North America. In each case, what changed? Climate.

It is clear that changes in climate will not be uniform across the landscape. Some locations will get hotter and drier and some will get cooler and wetter. Some areas will receive less snow in winter but more rain in the spring or fall, and so on. As a result, the changes to our forests will not be uniform. Different trees and different forests will react differently.

The Riverside Fire on Mount Hood National Forest in September 2020. Drought stress and sudden shifts in weather can combine to devastating effect.

PHOTO:
U.S. FOREST SERVICE

- Some species will benefit and expand their range, while others will suffer decline and lose their habitat to species better adapted to the new conditions.

- Changes in climate will influence the ability of tree seedlings to become established, and the ability of both young and mature trees to survive in a given location. Some trees will be able to adapt, while others will suffer stress and die due to pathogens and increased attacks from insects, such as bark beetles, that attack drought-stressed trees.

- Wildfires are predicted to increase as temperatures rise and forest fuels dry out sooner in the spring and remain dry longer into the fall.

This combination of factors will likely result in a rearranging of Northwest forests. Some may move northward, some may move up mountains (or to a different side). Some, like those that prefer mountaintops, may lose their habitat altogether.

Some of our older forests may lose the habitat in which they developed and experience losses to wildfire, windthrow, and insects and disease. They will be replaced by younger, early successional forests, or by different species of trees better adapted to the new conditions.

The catastrophic wildfires that ravaged the Northwest in the summer of 2020 provide an example of how a changing climate and forests under drought stress can combine for widespread and potentially long-term changes to Northwest forests.

How our forests adapt remains to be seen.

Although it is likely that temperatures in the Northwest will increase in coming years, it is less certain what will happen with precipitation. Less precipitation would likely magnify the effects of warmer growing seasons, resulting in more prolonged summer droughts. Warmer, wetter winters may occur, but that increase in precipitation may be offset by reduced snowpack, which many plant species depend on for moisture during the spring and early summer.

The seasonality of precipitation could also shift. If we get more rainfall during early summer, that could increase foliage diseases such as needle casts and blights in conifers, and anthracnose and other leaf diseases in broadleaves. Increased summer rainfall in central British Columbia has already facilitated a major foliage disease outbreak in lodgepole pine. In the northeastern United States, the same has happened to eastern white pine. Swiss needle cast in western Oregon and Washington is associated with the coastal fog and low cloud zone within about 30 miles of the Pacific Ocean. If late spring and early summer rainfall significantly increase across this region, Swiss needle cast could also increase, resulting in defoliation and weakening of Douglas-firs.

So, how, specifically, do these concepts apply to current conversations about how Northwest forests might react to changing climates? Frustratingly for many of us, the answers are not totally clear. That's because we're uncertain of exactly how, or how fast, our climate is likely to change, and also because the changes are not likely to be

Although it is likely that temperatures in the Northwest will increase in coming years, it is less certain what will happen with precipitation.

uniform over widely dispersed locations. And our mountainous landscapes dramatically influence the complexity of the situation. Slope, aspect, hillslope position, microtopography, cold air drainage, and the pooling and settling of cold air in bottoms and canyons all influence the trees that grow there. Therefore, climate-caused mortality on mountains is likely to appear patchy, as certain locations experience extreme climate events that might not occur in other locations.

Climate-related changes are now occurring on every continent. These changes include climate impacts, such as warming and drought; losses in habitat for plants and animals; air and water pollution; and increasing impact from invasive species. Invasive species from other continents in particular have the potential to profoundly influence forests of the Pacific Northwest — in fact, we have already experienced some of those impacts. Major invasive species impacting Northwest forests include:

- White pine blister rust (Asian then European), which weakens and kills all five-needle pines in North America.

- Sudden Oak Death (European), which kills tanoak and several species of West Coast oaks.

- Port-Orford-Cedar root disease (non-native planting stock) threatens the existence of Port-Orford-cedar.

- The balsam woolly adelgid (European) retards the growth of both grand fir and subalpine fir; the spruce aphid (European) causes needle loss and weakening in Sitka spruce along the coast.

- Although it's not yet been seen here, the risk to Northwest forests from the emerald ash borer (Asian) cannot be overstated. Current projections suggest this could eliminate Oregon ash from our landscapes.

- Gypsy moth (Asia), another serious invasive insect that attacks a variety of conifers, is routinely controlled in urban and semi-urban areas of the Northwest,

thanks to a joint state and federal monitoring program. Otherwise, it would have a devastating impact on our forests.

And so it goes. But in the end, forests are adaptable. As climate changes, some forests will expand their range, while others will contract. Some will move northward while others move southward. Some will move up the mountain slopes while others move down. Perhaps the biggest risks are from the increasing presence of large, catastrophic fires that come with hotter, drier conditions, and rapidly expanding insect and disease populations that become more virulent under new climatic conditions.

How do we adapt to these changes?

- By educating ourselves about the causes of climate change and its many impacts on Earth's ecosystems

- By doing what we can to reduce our own impacts on climate.

- By learning about interactions between climate change and our forests.

- By doing what we can to limit the spread and negative impacts of invasive species. This includes both plants and animals — on land and in our waters.

- By learning what constitutes healthy forests (especially biodiversity) and what management techniques are likely to maintain healthy forests.

- By taking care not to introduce unplanned fires into our forests.

Action on the global scale often seems too overwhelming for many of us to undertake, but we can all look for actions that we can take at our local levels.

There are no easy answers to the question of how changing climates will impact Northwest forests. To better understand the situation and work toward solutions, we need to think about complex ecological systems reacting to complex ecological changes.

7 potential impacts of climate change on Northwest forests

We can only speculate on the specifics of how forests will adapt to changes in climate. Here are a few impacts to Northwest forests that experts suggest could result.

PHOTO: JANET DONNELLY, © OREGON STATE UNIVERSITY

Noble fir could lose cool, moist habitat in its southern range.

PHOTO: BILL KRUEGER © OREGON STATE UNIVERSITY

It will be harder for seedlings to survive longer periods of drought.

PHOTO: TRAVIS WOOLEY

Lodgepole pine trees killed by mountain pine beetle in Oregon.

Increase in oak habitat

1 Low-elevation forests in southwestern Oregon and the Willamette Valley now composed of mixed stands of Douglas-fir and Oregon white oak are already becoming more oak-dominated as the less drought-tolerant Douglas-fir suffers increased mortality from increased summer drought. Douglas-fir, in turn, may migrate up the mountain slopes, where conditions are cooler and more moist.

True fir migration

2 True firs that currently grow above the Douglas-fir zone across the Northwest may well migrate up the mountain slopes, seeking the cooler, more moist conditions that they prefer.

Loss of habitat for noble fir

3 Noble fir, whose southern limit in the Oregon Coast Range is currently found high atop Marys Peak, may well lose its cool, moist habitat. Warmer, drier conditions could result from decreases in fog and clouds that help mitigate summer drought. It is also threatened by potential losses in deep winter snowpacks, which facilitate the germination of its seeds. If this happens, noble fir might no longer be found atop Marys Peak, but only in Coast Range mountains farther to the north.

Change of address for Pacific silver fir

4 Pacific silver fir, whose lower elevational limit is set by the lowest limit of snowpack, may shift upslope or to northern aspects of the mountains if snows at the lower elevations decrease.

Warmer, drier soils

5 Fires in the lower elevation forests of eastern Oregon and Washington could result in higher soil temperatures and drier seedbeds, making it more difficult for trees that currently occupy those forests (especially lodgepole and ponderosa pines) to regenerate. This could pave the way for even wider expansion of more drought-tolerant junipers and high desert shrubs.

Some habitats become cooler and wetter

6 If high elevations become cooler and wetter, a few species like Alaska-cedar and Engelmann spruce that like cool, moist environments might move farther south than their current ranges. But if it becomes warmer and drier, they may retreat northward.

More die-offs

7 Widescale tree mortality may become more frequent, such as the die-off of ponderosa pine along the lower slopes of the Sierra Nevada Mountains of California due to severe drought and bark beetle attacks. And large die-offs increase the likelihood of large, devastating fires.

National Champion Trees of Oregon and Washington

The National Registry of Champion Trees has been maintained by an organization known as American Forests since 1940. An up-to-date listing is available at Americanforests.org. Champions are determined by a combined score, rather than a single criterion, like height or girth. Total points are determined by adding the circumference at breast height (in inches), the height (in feet) and one-quarter of the crown spread (in feet). If you're interested in measuring your own big trees and perhaps nominating them to be on the list, instructions are included on the website.

Two large, old Douglas-firs along the Hackleman Old Growth Trail on Tombstone Pass in western Oregon.

Scientific and common names appear in this list as they do on the American Forests website. They do not always correspond with those used in *Trees to Know in Oregon and Washington* and *Shrubs to Know in Pacific Northwest Forests*. The list includes trees (and sometimes large shrubs) that are either native or naturalized in Oregon and Washington. "Naturalized" means that the plants were first brought into the region by humans but have escaped cultivation and now survive on their own. The National Champion trees for some Northwestern species occur in adjoining states, especially California and Idaho; they are not included in this list.

The list below was compiled in November 2019 — the most recent available. As we all know, trees grow and trees die; many of the larger trees also lose their tops in high winds. So, this list changes with the years.

Genus	Species	Scientific name	Location	Points	Circum. (in)	Height (ft)	Spread (ft)
alder	red	*Alnus rubra*	Benton Co., OR	280	165	98	68
apple	Oregon crab	*Malus fusca*	King Co., WA	156	90	48	73.5
birch	European white	*Betula pendula*	Clackamas Co., OR	219	124	78	68
"cedar"	Alaska	*Cupressus nootkatensis*	Olympic National Park, WA	585	454	124	28
"cedar"	Port-Orford	*Chamaecyparis lawsoniana*	Coos Co., OR	773	522	242	35
"cedar"	incense	*Calocedrus decurrens*	Josephine Co., OR	633	484	138	45
cercocarpus	birchleaf	*Cercocarpus betuloides*	Douglas Co., OR	110	73	28	37
cherry	bitter	*Prunus emarginata*	Marion Co., OR	121	35	83	10
chestnut	American	*Castanea dentata*	Thurston Co., WA	354	237	93.5	94.67
chestnut	horse	*Aesculus hippocastanum*	King Co., WA	341	237	85.5	72.58
chokecherry	western	*Prunus virginiana*	Marion Co., OR	116	40	69	28
cottonwood	black	*Populus balsamifera*	Clallum Co., WA	421	252	148	82
cottonwood	black	*Populus balsamifera*	Polk Co., OR	544	379	141	96
cypress	Monterey	*Cupressus macrocarpa*	Douglas Co., OR	605	483	101	85
dogwood	western	*Cornus sericea*	Polk Co., OR	66	29	26	44

Douglas-fir	coast	*Pseudotsuga menziesii*	Lake Quinault, Olympic National Park, WA	891	581	293.67	66.25
elder	blue	*Sambucus cerulea*	Linn Co., OR	170	122	39	35
elder	blackbead	*Sambucus melanocarpa*	Clackamas Co., OR	56	26	22	32
fir	noble	*Abies procera*	Gifford Pinchot National Forest, WA	579	316	251.67	44
fir	grand	*Abies grandis*	Clallum Co., WA	504	265	227	48
fir	Pacific silver	*Abies amabilis*	Olympic National Park, WA	444	212	222	38
fir	Pacific silver	*Abies amabilis*	Olympic National Park, WA	446	216	220	38
fir	subalpine	*Abies lasiocarpa*	Olympic National Park, WA	384	252	125	26
hawthorn	black	*Crataegus douglasii*	Liberty Co. WA	140	84	45	42
hazelnut	Turkish	*Corylus colura*	Benton Co., OR	232	136	80	63
hemlock	western	*Tsuga heterophylla*	Olympic National Park, WA	546	343	190	50
hemlock	mountain	*Tsuga mertensiana*	Yakima Co., WA	428	325	89	57
juniper	western	*Juniperus occidentalis*	Lake Co., OR	312	233	68	44
larch	subalpine	*Larix lyallii*	Wenatchee National Forest, WA	391	268	104	75
laurelcherry	English	*Prunus laurocerasus*	King Co., WA	163	116.4	32.25	56.33
maple	Rocky mountain	*Acer glabrum*	Island Co., WA	196	121	62	51
maple	bigleaf	*Acer macrophyllum*	Lane Co., OR	605	463	119	91
maple	vine	*Acer circinatum*	Clatsop Co., OR	127	74	43	39
oak	English	*Quercus robur*	Thurston Co., WA	382	238	118	104
oak	Oregon white	*Quercus garryana*	Multnomah Co., OR	408	288	97	91
pine	Austrian	*Pinus nigra*	King Co., WA	266	150	102.42	55
pine	ponderosa	*Pinus ponderosa*	Deschutes Co., OR	532	348	166.76	68
pine	lodgepole (Rocky mountain)	*Pinus contorta latifolia*	Grant Co., OR	257	136	110	44
pine	knobcone	*Pinus attenuata*	Josephine Co., OR	248	118	117	51
pine	shore	*Pinus contorta contorta*	Bryant Co., WA	286	152	124	40
plum	Indian	*Oemleria cerasiformis*	Marion Co., OR	51	20	26	18
redcedar	western	*Thuja plicata*	Clallum Co., WA	922	746	163.67	48
sagebrush	big	*Artemisia tridentata*	Jefferson Co., OR	53	32	16	18
serviceberry	western	*Amelanchier alnifolia*	Clackamas Co., OR	87	37	44	25
silktassel	wavyleaf	*Garrya elliptica*	Curry Co., OR	76	49	22	18
spruce	Sitka	*Picea sitchensis*	Olympic National Park, WA	951	740	191	80
spruce	Engelmann	*Picea engelmanii*	Clackamas Co., OR	394	260	127	27
sumac	smooth	*Rhus glabra*	King Co., WA	69	26	35.42	29.5
tamarisk	small-flower	*Tamarix paryiflora*	Multnomah Co., OR	112	80	24	32
willow	Scouler	*Salix scouleriana*	Columbia Co., OR	228	162	54	48
willow	Pacific	*Salix lucida lasiandra*	Washington Co., OR	191	102	70	74
willow	northwest	*Salix sessilifolia*	Marion Co., OR	76	29	42	21
yew	Pacific	*Taxus brevifolia*	Gifford Pinchot National Forest, WA	250	182.5	60	30

Western hemlocks commonly germinate atop stumps and logs, but need to sink their roots into the soil to sustain themselves.

A chipmunk munches a cone in the boughs of subalpine fir.

INDEX

Hesperocyparis macnabiana 21
Hesperocyparis macrocarpa 119
Hesperocyparis pigmaea 22
Hesperocyparis sargentii 23
Hinds walnut 114
holly 130
honeylocust 131
Hooker willow 116
horse-chestnut 85, 126

I

Ilex 130
incense-cedar 27, 29, 144, 149, 151

J

Japanese-cedar 123
Japanese maples 133
Jeffrey pine 46, 47, 144
Jensen, Ed 172
Juglans 114, 136
 Juglans hindsii 114
 Juglans nigra 136
 Juglans regia 136
juniper 36, 163
Juniperus 36
 Juniperus maritima 37
 Juniperus occidentalis 38
 Juniperus scopulorum 37
 Juniperus virginiana 37

K

Kalapuya Indians 155
keys 17, 75
Klamath plum 90, 92
knobcone pine 47, 48, 144
Kousa dogwood 128

L

larch 39
Larix 39
 Larix lyallii 40
 Larix occidentalis 40
Libocedrus decurrens 29
limber pine 51, 52
Liquidambar styraciflua 135

Some broadleaves, like these ashes and cottonwoods along the Columbia River, tolerate high water levels; others don't.

Liriodendron tulipifera 137
Lithocarpus 112
 Lithocarpus densiflorus 113
locust 131
lodgepole pine 43, 44, 149, 150, 151, 153, 163
Lombardy or black poplar 135

M

madrones 101
Malus 80
 Malus fusca 81
aple 102, 132
McNab's cypress 21
Mendocino cypress 22
Menzies, Archibald 155
Metasequoia glyptostroboides 120
mixed-conifer forests 144
Modoc cypress 21
monkey puzzle 121
Monterey cypress 119
mountain-ash 133
mountain hemlock 33, 34, 151
ountain-mahoganies 106
mugo pine 122

N

National Champion Trees of
 Oregon and Washington 164
national forests 157
national monuments 157
national parks 157
National Registry of Champion
 Trees 164
Native broadleaved trees 74
Native conifers 18
noble fir 63-66, 71, 151, 163
Nootka-cedar 28
Nootka-cypress 28
Northern red oak 133
Northwest forests 138
northwest willow 116
Norway maple 132
Notholithocarpus 112
 Notholithocarpus densiflorus 113

O

oak 108, 133
oleaster 134
Oregon ash 82, 148

Acorn woodpeckers stash their food supply in the creviced bark of an old Oregon white oak.

Wind-blown sand and ice often blast the buds off one side of trees growing at treeline, as in these Engelmann spruce.

Burls on Sitka spruce in Olympic National Park, Washington. Burls form as a result of insects, disease or damage.

About the author

Ed Jensen was raised amid the rich farmlands and wooded hills of northwestern Illinois. His love of forests began with a summer job in Olympic National Park during his college years. There he found inspiration in the awesome majesty and subtle beauty of old-growth Douglas-fir/western hemlock forests. His life was forever changed.

Ed has spent his entire career teaching students at Oregon State University about forests and the trees, shrubs and native plants that compose them. His enthusiasm for teaching has been recognized with numerous awards and is reflected in several books in addition to this one: *Woody Plants in North America, Shrubs to Know in Pacific Northwest Forests* and the *Manual of Oregon Trees and Shrubs*. Most importantly, his love of forests has resulted in endearing relationships with thousands of students.